UNKNOWN ITALY

★ ★

The Cities of Central Italy

Other translations in English of the author's travel books

UNKNOWN FRANCE	:	FROM PARIS TO THE RIVIERA
		THE FRENCH ALPS : THE RIVIERA
		THE ROADS TO SPAIN
		THE VALLEY OF THE LOIRE : BRITTANY
UNKNOWN SPAIN	:	SPAIN OF THE CONQUISTADORS (Northern Spain)
UNKNOWN ITALY	:	THE ITALIAN LAKES AND ALPINE REGIONS

In preparation

UNKNOWN SPAIN	:	SOUTH
UNKNOWN ITALY	:	SOUTH

LIST OF ILLUSTRATIONS

AUTHOR'S PREFACE

This second volume of itineraries through Italy takes you first from Milan to Bologna, then from that city and from Sarzana on the coast to Florence, and from there by three different routes to Rome. It covers the provinces of Tuscany, Umbria, and Latium.

As in my previous volume the well-known art cities are side by side with those which are less known, but I have set myself rather to introduce you to cities and to buildings that are usually neglected by tourists. I have not described either Florence or Rome, which need each a volume to themselves, but I have taken my readers in other well-known cities such as Lucca, Siena or Perugia to the more neglected buildings and monuments, while I have also introduced cities which should be better known such as Todi, Gubbio or San Gimignano.

There is, of course, no need for the tourist to keep to the same itinerary. A study of the table at the start of the book will enable him to change from one to the other at his convenience.

GEORGES PILLEMENT

PARIS

LIST OF ITINERARIES

I—300 kilometres

FROM MILAN TO BOLOGNA

ABBEY OF CHIARAVALLE — ABBEY OF VIBOLDONE —
MELEGNANO — LODI — PIACENZA — GROPPARELLO —
VELLEIA — VIGOLO MARCHESE — CASTELL'ARQUATO —
ABBEY OF CHIARAVALLE DELLA COLOMBA — FIDENZA —
FONTANELLATO — CASTEL GUELFO — PARMA —
TORRECHIARA — REGGIO — MODENA — NONANTOLA —
SALA BOLOGNESE — BOLOGNA

On this itinerary, which leads from the north into central Italy we find many of the best known art cities of the Italian peninsula, which are as rich in their religious and secular buildings as they are in their museums. There are also several abbeys which we should not fail to see, notably the two of Chiaravalle. Other features are several attractive small towns, such as Castell'Arquato; mediaeval castles such as Castel Guelfo and Fontanellato; and the Cathedral of Fidenza, which is remarkable for the Romanesque sculptures of its façade.

II—150 kilometres

FROM SARZANA TO LUCCA AND FLORENCE

FOSDINOVO — CARRARA — MASSA — PIETRASANTA —
LUCCA — MARLIA — SEGROMIGNO — CAMIGLIANO S.
GEMMA — S. GENNARO — COLLODI — VILLA BASILICA
— PESCIA — CASTELVECCHIO — UZZANO — BUGGIANO
CASTELLO — ALTOPASCIO — FUCECCHIO — S. MINIATO
— EMPOLI — MONTELUPO FIORENTINO

Instead of following the sea coast this detour goes among the mountains past the fortfiied castle of Fosdinovo and the town of Carrara, famous for its marble and its Romanesque cathedral. The itinerary will introduce us to the unique ensemble of Romanesque and Gothic buildings at Lucca, and in the surroundings several interesting Romanesque churches and fine villas with superb gardens. Then we visit S. Miniato and Empoli, two towns of unusual character.

III—200, 175 and 150 kilometres

FROM LA SPEZIA, MODENA AND BOLOGNA TO FLORENCE BY WAY OF PISTOIA

AULLA — CASTELNUOVO — BARGA — LOPPIA — COREGLIA — BORGO — DIECIMO — BAGNI DI LUCCA — S. CASSIANO — S. MARCELLO — SASSUOLO — SPILAM- BERTO — VIGNOLA — PIEVE TREBBIO — MARZABOTTO — PISTOIA — PRATO — POGGIO A CAIANO — SIGNA

These three itineraries, which join at Pistoia, enable us to see Pistoia and Prato, two interesting Tuscan towns with remarkable cathedrals, various churches and first-class monuments, then several small Tuscan towns of secondary interest, like Barga, remarkable castles, like that of Vignola, and attractive Romanesque churches.

IV—275 kilometres

FROM FLORENCE TO PESARO

PONTASSIEVE — VALLOMBROSA — CASTELLO DI ROMENA — S. PIETRO DI ROMENA — POPPI — CAMAL- DOLI — BIBBIENA — LA VERNA — SANSEPOLCRO — URBINO — FOSSOMBRONE — FANO

This itinerary across the Marches towards the Adriatic passes through such wonderful art cities as Poppi, Sansepolcro and above all

ogival arcades are supported by twin slender columns. From
the cloister there is a fine view over the right side of the
church and the steeple, which was erected in 1568 on the
side of the façade.

On the right is the 14th-century refectory and the 18th-
century Abbatial Palace which were incorporated into these
rural constructions.

There was good reason to restore the Abbey of Chiaravalle,
which I saw several years ago in a pitiful condition, but why
go to the point of erecting new buildings alongside the ancient
ones?

Let us return to the N.9, then leave it again after five
kilometres in order to see, immediately on the right, THE
ABBEY OF VIBOLDONE which was founded by the
Umiliati in the 12th century and mentioned in a Bull of
Innocent III in 1201. It subsequently passed into the hands
of the Olivetains who remained there until 1777.

Begun in 1176, work on the church was continued
throughout the 13th century, while the façade was erected in
the 14th century. Built of brick in the Lombard style, it
presents Romanesque and Gothic elements. A large marble
oculus surmounted by a twin window is situated above a fine
marble portal whose tympanum, with the two aedicules
flanking it, is embellished with statues by an unknown
Master, originally from Campione, known as the Master of
Viboldone. Some engaged columns serving as buttresses
separate the central part of the Gothic bays which ensure
light for the side-aisles and which are surmounted by purely
decorative twin windows. Behind the church, above the apse,
rises a beautiful 13th-century campanile which was completed in the 14th century. It is pierced by simple, double and
triple bays and crowned by a conical steeple.

The interior has three naves separated by columns which
support the semicircular arcades; the vaulting is ogival.
The church was decorated throughout with frescoes part of

which remain. Those of the right nave date from the second half of the 14th century and are by Giovanni da Milano. Those of the left nave, dating from the same period, are by a late pupil of Giotto, while in the choir a *Last Judgment* and a *Madonna on a Throne Between Saints* are by an immediate pupil of Giotto (1349) whose work is outstanding for the grandeur of the composition and the force of expression.

The abbatial buildings, now occupied by the Benedictines, have beautiful Renaissance windows.

Of interest also is a third and more modest abbey, the ABBEY OF MIRADOLE which we can see between the two preceding ones, above Opera. Founded in the 13th century, it presents a partly disfigured late 14th-century church with a single nave with timbered vaulting and a square choir decorated with a large 15th-century fresco. Alongside, a small cloister from the first half of the 15th century is surmounted on two sides by a loggia with slender columns.

We next pass MELEGNANO where the Visconti had a castle. It was built in 1350 by Bernardo Visconti, who was very fond of it, and so too was Gian Galeazzo. In 1532 it passed into the hands of Medeghino who enlarged it. In modern times it has been less gently treated, and is now used partly as municipal offices and partly as dwellings. We can see two massive towers and, on the first floor, which is reached by a staircase available for horses, some 16th-century frescoes.

Finally, there is the Church of Prepositurale, which was founded in the 4th century, rebuilt in 1418 and has three naves; also the graceful small Baroque Church of S. Rocco.

We continue across a wonderfully irrigated plain and reach LODI, an agricultural and industrial centre on the right bank of the Adda. The ancient city, the former Roman *Laus Pompeia*, lies six kilometres farther on. After its destruction by the Milanese in 1158, the town was rebuilt on its present site on the initiative of Frederick Barbarossa. We reach

Piazza della Vittoria, the centre of the town, where we find
the Cathedral which was erected after 1158. The façade,
which has been remodelled at various times, lacks unity.
The portal is decorated with late 12th-century sculptures
with, on the tympanum, *Christ, the Virgin and Saint Bassiano*
and, on the jambs, *Adam and Eve*. The Gothic porch dates
from the 15th century and the lions belonged to the ancient
11th-century Cathedral of *Laus Pompeia*. The large rose-
window is of 1560 and the Renaissance double bay alongside
the portal with candelabrum-like slender columns is of 1509.
Of interest also is the elegant niche with a copper gilt statue
of Saint Bassiano of 1285. On the right side of the façade
rises a massive, unfinished campanile by Callisto Piazza
(1539).

The interior, in the basilican plan with three naves separated by pillars, was remodelled in the 18th century. The
choir is raised above a vast crypt where we can see some
8th- and 9th-century bas-reliefs. There are two other Roman
bas-reliefs in the left nave. The Courtyard of the Canons has
one side dating from the 13th century and the other from the
14th century.

On the left of the Cathedral, the *Broletto* has an 18th-
century façade with busts of Gnaius Pompeius Strabo,
benefactor of ancient *Laus Pompeia*, and of Frederick Barbarossa who founded the new town of Lodi. Passing beneath
an arcade we enter Piazza Broletto, where we can see the
16th-century baptismal fonts of the Cathedral transformed
into a fountain. On the right is the lateral façade of the
Cathedral, with a 12th-century portal and, at the far end,
the archivolts and the window decorated with Renaissance
terracottas of the Treasure of S. Bassiano. We find the same
decoration on Piazza del Mercato, where we see the exterior
of the 12th-century apse of the Cathedral and, alongside, the
Bishop's Palace by Veneroni (1730) with a beautiful unfinished Doric courtyard by the Sirtori brothers.

We will return to Piazza della Vittoria and, taking the street on the left, we reach the Sanctuary of the Incoronata, a beautiful Renaissance construction undertaken in 1488 by Giovanni Battagio. The campanile of 1503 is by Maggi.

In the centre of the façade is a portico with three arcades fronted by a fine Renaissance portal of 1490. The octagonal interior has two storeys and is surmounted by a cupola. The architectural structure and decoration are in the Bramantesque style of Battagio. The decoration of the ground floor is by the Castillo brothers and by the Piazza. In the Chapel of S. Paolo are four panels by Bergognone dating from his finest period and relating to *The Life of the Virgin*.

We can also see in the Corso Umberto I, the 18th-century Church of S. Filippo alongside a Baroque palace of the same name built by Sirtori; it houses the library and the museum, and, above all, the Lombard-Gothic Church of S. Francesco which was founded in 1289 and finished in the 14th century. The unfinished brick façade has an ogival portico surmounted by a rose-window and two twin windows.

The interior, in the form of a Latin cross, has three naves separated by massive columns which support the ogival vaulting. The columns are decorated with 14th- and 15th-century frescoes by local painters.

Alongside, the Ospedale Maggiore, which was begun in 1459 and enlarged in 1571 from the design by Pellegrini, was given a façade by Piermarini in 1792. The most ancient part consists of a beautiful courtyard of 1473 with porticos and loggia, stone columns and archivolts, and terracotta medallions. The vaulting of a large room is decorated with landscapes and masks by Ferrari (1593).

Six kilometres to the west lies LODI VECCHIO, the ancient Roman town of *Laus Pompeia* where the Supervisor of Antiquities of Lombardy has undertaken excavations; also the remains of the mediaeval town which was destroyed in 1158. It is now a village which has preserved at least the

Basilica of S. Bassiano which was founded in 378, re-erected
in the 10th century and again in the 14th century. The façade
dates from the last period. The interior has three naves
separated by pillars with crudely sculptured capitals, and
some remains of 14th-century frescoes.

Returning to Lodi, we take the N.9 which after little more
than a kilometre passes the Church of S. Bernardo degli
Olivetani, the choir of which is decorated with fine stalls by
Fra Giovanni da Verona, who died in 1523.

We continue along a straight road and, after crossing the
Po, reach Piacenza.

PIACENZA is one of the art cities which the tourist
wrongly neglects in favour of others more famous. He glances
at the Cathedral and the Gothic Palace and ignores an
ensemble of interesting churches and palaces.

Piazza dei Cavalli lies in the centre of the town. It owes its
name to the two equestrian statues of the Farnese which
stand in front of the Palazzo del Comune. These two
vigorous works are among the masterpieces of Baroque
statuary. The one on the left represents Duke Alessandro
Farnese and the one on the left his son, Ranuccio I.

The Palazzo del Commune itself, commonly known as the
Gotico, is a masterpiece of 13th-century Lombard architecture and is one of the finest public palaces in Italy. It was
begun in 1280. The façade presents on the ground floor a
deep portico with two ogival vaulted naves with five large
tierspoint arcades in front and two on each side. Above,
six large semicircular windows with rich terracotta decoration enclose triple or quadruple bays with, in the centre,
a *Virgin and Child*, a 13th-century Lombard work. The
whole is crowned by Ghibelline crenels with three small
turrets. The courtyard is worth a glance, as it is quite
picturesque.

Opposite, the ancient Governor Palace was rebuilt in 1781
by Lotario Tomba. Behind, on the square of the same name,

is the Church of S. Francesco, which was begun in 1278 thanks to the generosity of Ubertino Landi. The façade, which is still Lombard in its structure but Gothic in its form, decorated with elegant terracotta pinnacles, presents a fine splayed portal with twisted columns and, on the tympanum, *Saint Francis Receiving the Stigmata* by the School of Amadeo (about 1470). The right side is hidden by houses, but we can see the beautiful apse with its blind arcades and Lombard campanile.

The purely Gothic interior has three naves separated by large ogival arcades supported by cylindrical pillars. The polygonal apse is enclosed by an ambulatory with radiating chapels.

Via XX Settembre leads to the Cathedral, which was begun in 1122 and finished in 1233. It is a wonderful Lombard construction with, for the last period, some Gothic elements. The façade has the exuberant character which we find in many Italian cathedrals with their profusion of blind arcades, porticos and loggias. Here the arcades have a particularly happy arrangement. Some follow the upward sweep of the gable and the row which surmounts to right and to left the two lateral porches with loggias. In the centre, the porch and the loggia are higher and are surmounted by a large rose-window. Two round columns which act as buttresses divide the façade into three sections and extend as far as the upper gallery. The whole is very harmonious.

The columns of the central porch are supported by lions which belong to a Renaissance restoration. The architrave of the portal is supported by two 12th-century figures representing *Usury* and *Avarice*. The left portal, the work of a pupil of Wiligelmo and Nicolo, is decorated with symbols of the *Virtues* and *Vices*, while on the architrave we can recognise *Scenes from The Life of the Virgin*. The right portal presents on the architrave *Six Scenes from The Life of Christ* by a pupil of Nicolo.

Colorno. In the left transept we can see the monument of Margaret of Austria.

The monastery, which has been transformed into barracks, dates from the second half of the 16th century. On the ground floor there is a large cloister with a gallery.

We next head for Via di Campagna where we find the Church of la Madonna di Campagna, which is one of the most interesting examples of Renaissance art in Italy. It was built between 1522 and 1528 and remodelled in 1791 by the extension of the choir. It is built in the form of a Greek cross with small angle chapels. Over the centre rises a high lantern-turret pierced by windows and surmounted by a gallery.

In the arm of the entrance we see the masterpiece of Solaro (1543), a fresco portraying *Saint George Destroying the Dragon*. On the left is a fine fresco by Pordenone, his first work at Piacenza (1525), portraying *Saint Augustine*. The frescoes of the cupola are by Solaro and Pordenone. The stalls in the choir are by Giulio Bossi (1560). The frescoes of the third and fourth angle chapels are by Pordenone.

Alongside, the ancient monastery of the Olivetains, now the civil hospital, consists of a small 15th-century cloister with gracefully-decorated arcades and a large cloister with granite columns. Both are attributed to Bramante.

We leave Piacenza through the Porta Roma, but instead of following the Via Emilia (N.9) we take, on the right, the road to Castell'Arquato which, after leaving the sandy bed of the Nure, passes through S. GIORGIO PIACENTINO where a large castle flanked by a tower has become the Town Hall and where, in the midst of a large park, we can see the Villa Gazzola of 1610 attributed to Vignola.

We next pass through CARPANETO PIACENTINO where again the castle has been transformed into the Town Hall after having been totally disfigured.

We can see a third castle, much more impressive, by following the road which, some distance before Carpaneto, heads for **GROPPARRELLO**. It once belonged to the Bishops of Piacenza, to the Farnese and to the Anguissola. It rises on a rock whose irregular form it follows. The façade has been restored and a drawbridge leads to the entrance tower. It is flanked by several towers and in the centre rises the square keep. In the interior we can see an interesting armoury.

A small road enables us to reach *Velleia*, which is the most important archaeological centre of Emilia. After having been a Ligurian town, it became a Roman *municipium* when it developed into a health resort. The town disappeared in the early 4th century.

It was in 1747 that the fortunate discovery of the celebrated *Alimentary Table* of Trajan, the most important historical document of that period, drew attention to Velleia. Excavations undertaken in 1760 by the order of Philip of Parma, disclosed an amphitheatre, a basilica and a forum; also numerous marble and bronze sculptures, inscriptions and various objects which were transported to the Museum of Parma. Other excavations were undertaken in the 19th century and in our own century, and the ruins have been tastefully restored.

The centre of the ruins is occupied by the Forum which has preserved its paving. It was enclosed by a portico of which two columns have recently been re-erected. On the north side existed a raised edifice which was the Temple, with four Corinthian columns on its façade. Two smaller buildings were probably the *curia* and the Magistrates' Room. The Basilica stood on the south side: it was the principal edifice of the town and was embellished with 12 statues of Emperors.

Finally, on the west side there were private dwellings and on the south-west side the baths. On the south-east side we can see the remains of the Amphitheatre.

The objects discovered during excavations have been installed in a small museum.

We next reach VIGOLO MARCHESE where we can see a baptistery of 1008. It is circular in plan enclosed by blind arcades on the exterior, with three apsidioles and a cupola which, on the exterior, is supported by six columns. In the centre, the baptismal vat has been hewn out of a wonderful capital which dates from the Imperial period. The ancient 11th-century Church of S. Giovanni Battista, partly restored, with its high steeple, consists of three naves which are separated by columns which support the pointed arcades, and terminate in a semicircular apse.

We skirt the hill and reach CASTELL'ARQUATO, one of those small Italian towns which a tourist discovers with joy. Castell'Arquato deserves to be better known, for an *ensemble* of rare monuments have been discovered there in a setting which moreover has not yet been commercialised. I recommend the restaurant at the top of the town and the hotel lower down. If incidentally, to visit this place, we do not want to make the detour by way of Velleia, we can easily go there along the Via Emilia and take a short side road.

The town was mentioned as early as 566 and, after having been owned by the Bishop of Piacenza, it was raised to a Commune at the close of the 13th century under the seigniory of Alberto Scoto who was succeeded by the Visconti.

The town lies on the slopes of a hill with the Arda Torrent at its foot. We first find the Torrione Farnesiano, a late 16th-century construction on a square plan with a high arcade crowned with a loggia, then the Palazzo del Duca, a 13th- and 14th-century construction, rebuilt in the 15th century, with terracotta ornaments beneath which there is a fountain of 1292.

The road ascends, leaving, on the left, the Church of S. Pietro with a terracotta decorated Gothic portal, and we pass beneath the vaulting of a modern palace which is an imitation of a mediaeval castle, leaving, on the left, the

Oratory of S. Stefano and, on the right, the Baroque Church of the Trinity.

The road continues to ascend and we reach the *piazza* at the summit of the hill which is surrounded by all the interesting monuments of Castell'Arquato: the Town Hall, the Collegiate Church and the Castle.

The Palazzo Pretorio or Town Hall is a massive, picturesque, crenellated construction of 1293, with a covered outer flight of steps, an early 14th-century pentagonal tower, and a portico with loggia which was added in the 15th century. The windows have a beautiful terracotta decoration.

Opposite, fronted by a portico, is the Romanesque portal of the collegiate church with, on the tympanum, *The Virgin and Child Between Saint Peter and the Angel*, a 12th-century work by a pupil of Nicolo and its fine apse which gives on to the *piazza*.

The Collegiate Church is a Romanesque edifice of 1122, built on the ruins of an earlier church, which collapsed during the earthquake of 1117. It is in the basilican plan with three naves separated by pillars with beautiful historiated capitals with, in the principal nave, a timbered ceiling and it terminates in an oven-shaped apse with two apsidioles. The one on the right received a stucco decoration in the 18th century and is flanked by an apsidiole, much lower. The baptistery has preserved its 8th-century immersion vat and the walls are decorated with 14th-century frescoes. In the Chapel of Saint Catherine we can see other frescoes which date from the 15th century, a Romanesque *Christ on the Cross* and two Romanesque sculptures representing the Archangels Gabriel and Raphael.

At the other end of the square, the Rocca, which until recently has been used as a prison, will soon be restored. It is a powerful fortress with its crenellated towers and a high square keep. It was built by the Commune of Piacenza in 1343 and its defences were strengthened by Luchino Visconti in 1347.

I. PIACENZA, CATHEDRAL.

2. CASTELL'ARQUATO, PALAZZO
PRETORIO

bastion of the Guelf party to which it owes its present name. Built on a square plan with angle towers and a rich interior decoration, it has been very much restored.

If we are in no hurry, we can make another small detour in order to see a third fortress of Emilia by taking the road on the right, opposite the one to Fontanellato, which leads to NOCETO, only two kilometres away.

Of the castle there remains notably a massive and impressive keep on a rectangular plan with two storeys of machicolation, surmounted by watch paths with semicircular windows.

We return to the N.9 and reach PARMA, the most important city of Emilia after Bologna. Its university was famous and has preserved a group of very interesting monuments. The city was named *Julia* under Julius Caesar and *Augusta* under Augustus, then *Chrysopolis* under the Byzantines. It formed a Lombard duchy in the Middle Ages. Then in 1805 it became an independent Commune; from 1545 it had formed a duchy under the Farnese and later, the Bourbons.

We enter Piazza S. Croce where begins the large rectilinear street leading to the centre of the city and at the entrance to which we see, on the right, the Romanesque Church of S. Croce erected in 1210, modified in 1515 and altered in the 18th century. The apse, the small oblong windows and the portal with its zoomorphic decoration date from the original construction.

The interior, which is in three naves, has some fine early 12th-century historiated capitals of marble.

We will leave, on the left, the long façade of the Hospital of the Misericord which was founded about 1214, was rebuilt in the 15th and 16th centuries and is now used as the Archives Museum.

We next find, on the right, the Church of the Annunziata which was built in 1566 by Fornovo with a cupola of 1632 by Rainaldi and a Baroque façade. The interior, in an elliptical plan with large fluted columns, is enclosed by chapels with Baroque stucco decoration.

We cross the Parma and reach the picturesque Piazza Garibaldi, the centre of the city, with its façade of the Governor's Palace of 1760. At the angle of the square, where the Via della Republica begins, we can see the Palazzo del Municipio with its portico, begun by Magnani in 1627.

At the far end of the square is the Church of S. Pietro Apostolo, the most ancient building in Parma after the Cathedral, since it was founded before 955 but remodelled at the close of the 15th century, then rebuilt with a new orientation in 1710. The present façade of 1761 is by Petitot.

Let us take Via Cavour with, at No. 11, the Oratory of S. Lucia, rebuilt at the close of the 17th century with a façade by Oddi; then finally we reach Piazza del Duomo which best evokes memories of Parma's bygone days.

The Cathedral is a remarkable Romanesque edifice, which existed as early as 1046, but which was largely destroyed by an earthquake in 1117 and rebuilt according to a different design. The campanile dates from 1284 and the chapels on the right were added the following year, while those on the left were added in the 14th century.

The façade is very simple with its three series of blind semicircular arcades, the last one following the slope of the roof. In the centre, the principal portal is fronted by a portico built in 1281 by Giambono da Bissone, whose columns are supported by two lions. On the arch mouldings and on the architrave are *The Months of the Year* and some graceful bunches of grapes with figurines, including *A Centaur Pointing an Arrow at a Stag*. The doors were carved by Bianchino in 1494. On the right, the Gothic campanile decorated with trilobulate arcades is crowned with pinnacles and surmounted by a pyramidal spire.

The interior of the Cathedral is austere and impressive. It is in the form of a Latin cross with three naves separated

The arcades of the first chapels on the left are decorated with frescoes by Parmesan.

In the ancient Benedictine Monastery we can see two beautiful 16th-century cloisters, the library and the pharmacy and, somewhat farther on, the large Gothic Church of S. Francesco del Prato which was begun in 1260. A second period of building dates from 1398 and the third from 1445. The façade, which was erected in 1398 by Fra Giovanni Quaglia, has a fine Venetian-like portal and a wonderful rose-window of red marble in a terracotta-enclosed niche. The campanile is of 1516. The interior is not accessible.

We next reach the Palazzo della Pilotta, so called because one of its courtyards was devoted to the game known as *pilotta*. This is a colossal construction begun by the Farnese about 1583 with Boscoli as architect, resumed in 1602 with Campanini, but it has remained unfinished. The decoration of the windows towards Piazza della Ghiaia, where the façade was to have been erected, is by Battistelli.

The courtyard gives us an idea of the grandiose aspect the building would have had with its portico and two storeys surmounted by an attic.

The palace houses the National Museum of Antiquities, which was founded by Philip I of Bourbon in 1760 with the statues discovered during excavation at *Velleia* and was later completed with those which were discovered in 1844 in the Roman Theatre of Parma. It houses also the Palatine Library and the National Gallery which has a rich collection of paintings by Correggio, Carrache and Parmesan. This is one of those museums in Italy which we should not fail to visit.

We should also visit the Farnese Theatre which was built in 1618, inspired by the Olympic Theatre of Palladio. Someone will take us to the room of Correggio, in Via M. Melloni, in the suite of the Abbess of the Monastery of Saint Paul. Here in 1518 the artist decorated the dining-room, where figures of *Fortune, The Three Graces, Venus, Fauns* and *Cupids* create an utterly profane atmosphere which Stendhal especially appreciated, seeing in it the revelation of the feminine soul.

A room near by is decorated with frescoes by Araldi (1514) who also painted two other frescoes on the other side of the cloister in the cell of Saint Catherine.

The Royal Theatre was built in 1821 by Marie-Louise and, on the other side of the river, overlooking the Ducal Park now transformed into a public garden, is the Ducal Palace built for Ortavio Farnese by Boscoli in 1564 and modified by Petitot, who in 1767 built for angle pavilions. Several rooms have preserved their interesting 16th- and 17th-century frescoes in spite of the American bombardment in 1944.

There now remains to be seen the Church of S. Alessandro which was rebuilt by Magnani in 1622 and, above all, the Church of la Madonna della Steccata in the style of Bramante erected in 1521 by Zaccagni. It is an impressive construction in the form of a Greek cross with the four arms terminating in semicircular apses. In the centre rises a cupola adorned with a gallery and surmounted by a lantern-turret. There are many tombs, including that of Neipperg, the one-eyed general who followed Napoleon as Marie-Louise's lover. The cupola is decorated with a fresco by Gatti, while in the east arm we can see some frescoes by Anselami from the cartoons by Giulio Romano.

Before returning to the Via Emilia, we can see, ten kilometres to the south, the finest of all the castles in the Parma region, that of TORRECHIARA, which is proudly set on its hill and very well preserved. Built in 1448 by Pier Maria Rossi on a rectangular plan, it is surrounded by three *enceintes* with angle towers, watch-path and machicolation.

In the interior, a huge courtyard with a portico and a loggia on one side, has a terracotta decoration and graceful capitals. On the right of the entrance we can see a fresco of the second half of the 15th century, and in the chapel the tomb of Rossi and of his mistress, Bianca Pellegrini d'Arluno. On the upper floor, a large room with a decoration of masks by Baglione leads to the Golden Room, which was dedicated by Rossi to Bianca Pellegrini and splendidly decorated in 1463 by Bembo.

A few minutes away from Parma is the *Badia* which was built in 1471 by Ugolino Rossi, the natural son of Pier Maria Rossi. It was the seat of a monastery of monks from Monte Cassino and it is still a resting place for the Benedictines. In the church, which was rebuilt in the 18th century, we can see a late 15th-century fresco. A beautiful cloister dates from the 15th century.

We will return to Parma and take the Via Emilia which leads directly to REGGIO NELL'EMILIA, where we will stop at Piazza Battisti which is bordered by several palaces, including the Palazzo Busetti of 1671 attributed to Bernini. We reach the Cathedral which was built between 1285 and 1311 but subsequently remodelled, notably in the 15th century. The transept crossing with its three apses and the unfinished façade arranged in the classic style by Prospero Spani date from this latter period. To him we owe the two fine statues of *Adam* and *Eve*, inspired by Michelangelo, on the tympanum of the central portal. The same is true also of the large *Virgin and Child Between Donors* which decorates the tower.

The interior in the form of a Latin cross has three naves separated by pillars, barrel-vaulting, raised choir and three semicircular apses. In the third chapel on the right we can see the mausoleum of Valerio Malaguzzi by Prospero Spani, an *Assumption* by Guercino in the fourth chapel on the right, then in the treasure chamber a ciborium by Bartolo Spani and, in the crypt supported by 42 columns, a Roman mosaic.

Also on the square is the *Palazzo Comunale*, originally of 1414 but subsequently remodelled and enlarged, with its 18th-century portico.

We next see, on the *piazza* behind the Cathedral, the Basilica of S. Prospero which was founded in the 10th century, but rebuilt in 1514. The façade, added in 1748 by Cattani, is in a good Baroque style. It is flanked by a massive octagonal campanile with three orders which was erected in 1536 but left unfinished.

The interior, with three naves separated by large arcades supported by columns, is in the form of a Latin cross. We can see a beautiful sculptured pulpit of 1571 by Sampolo and some fine stalls of 1546 by Mantello. The choir and the apse are covered with frescoes by Procaccini with a *Last Judgment* and a *Descent from the Cross* inspired by Michelangelo. The transept has a *Christ Bearing His Cross* by Prospero Spani and a tomb by his uncle, Bartolomeo.

In Corso Garibaldi is the late 16th-century Church of la Madonna della Ghiaia by Balbi with its elegant brick façade with two orders. The interior in the form of a Greek cross with a large barrel-vaulted apse, a central cupola and four other cupolas on the chapels of the angle of the cross, is rather astonishing, not only for the harmony of its proportions but also for the wealth of its decorations. The frescoes are by Luca Ferrari, Gravasseti, Magnani and Tiarini. We must admire a fine *Christ on the Cross Consoled by an Angel* by Guerclino.

We must not overlook the Parmegiani Gallery with its 15th-century portal which was transported from Valencia, Spain, and its rich collections of Italian, French and Spanish art.

Of interest also are the Church of S. Girolamo, a curious construction by Vigarani, the Church of SS. Pietro e Prospero with its 18th-century façade and, alongside, the two 16th-century cloisters of the ancient Benedictine monastery and, here and there, numerous palaces, some by Spani.

Finally, we can see, three kilometres away, the villa known as Il Mauriziano where Ariosto was the guest of his cousins,

3. FIDENZA, DETAIL OF THE FACADE
OF THE CATHEDRAL.

4. LUCCA, CHURCH OF S. MICHELE

ITINERARY II

FROM SARZANA TO LUCCA AND FLORENCE

*Fosdinovo — Carrara — Massa — Pietrasanta — Lucca
— Marlia — Segromigno — Camigliano — S. Gennaro
— Collodi — Pescia — Castelvecchio — Uzzano —
Buggiano Castello — Altopascio — Fucecchio — S.
Miniato — Empoli — Montelupo Fiorentino.*

THE road along the Mediterranean coast passes through Liguria as far as Sarzana. We now enter Tuscany, but instead of continuing directly to Viareggio, we leave the Via Aurelia at the second intersection, then, on the left, take the road which heads for Fosdinovo across a hilly landscape with many olive groves.

We pass through Caniparola where we can see the 18th-century Villa Malaspina. The road begins to climb and we soon find the town of FOSDINOVO on a hill which is dominated by its spectacular castle. This stands on a rocky spur directly above the Magra and the Gulf of La Spezia. Built on an irregular plan, it is enclosed by high curtain walls and flanked by towers with, at the far end, an impressive circular keep with machicolation. The castle was acquired in 1340 by Malaspina whose tomb is in the Church of S. Remigio. It is a marble sarcophagus decorated with bas-reliefs and surmounted by a recumbent figure.

Shortly after Fosdinovo, there is a road, on the right, which follows the crest of the mountain and has fine views of the sea and often of the Apennines, and this leads us to CARRARA.

The marble of Carrara is world famous and has been used since ancient times. We can visit the quarries which are just beyond the town.

Carrara has several palaces, the most important of which is the Academy of Fine Arts alongside the keep of the ancient castle. It was built in the 16th century by Cybo-Malaspina as a ducal residence and in 1805 was offered to the Academy by Elisa Baciocchi.

In Via S. Maria there is a 16th-century house which was inhabited by Repetti, a naturalist and historian, and according to tradition, long before him by Petrarch in 1343. The marble façade, with three rectangular windows and architraves which are resting on elegant slender columns, has been influenced by Ligurian architecture.

We reach Piazza del Duomo which is embellished by a fountain and the statue of Andrea Doria, commonly known as the Giant, with the features of Neptune. This unfinished work is by Baccio Bandinelli.

Work on the cathedral began in the 11th century but did not advance very quickly. The apse was enlarged in the 13th century and its present design dates from the 14th. The exterior is entirely faced with bands of black and white marble. It is Romanesque as far as the first storey and the rest is Gothic.

The façade in the Pisan style is divided into two rows. The lower one is decorated with semicircular blind arcades and has a handsome portal which is flanked by pilasters and engaged columns with historiated capitals. On the semicircular arching there are animals rampant. The upper row has a wonderful rose-window in a coffer rectangle which is framed by an elegant Gothic loggia.

The semicircular apse is no less remarkable with its three tierspoint windows, the central one decorated with a marble figurine, and its loggia. On the right, the campanile, which is typically Ligurian, dates from the second half of the 13th century.

The interior, which we enter through a fine Romanesque portal on the right side, has three naves which are separated by columns having different capitals. On the walls are the remains of frescoes from the 12th and 14th centuries. Several works of art are outstanding, notably the choir screen, the pulpit and a *Virgin with Two Saints* both sculptured by Moschino.

We return to the N.1 at Avenza and continue to MASSA where we can start our visit by making a left turn on reaching Piazza Puccini. From there we reach Piazza Aranci embellished by its obelisk fountain with four lions built by Duchess Maria Beatrice, the daughter of Maria Theresa, and on three sides its two rows of orange trees. On the right, the Palazzo Cybo-Malaspina was the residence of the rulers of the town. Begun by Alberico I Cybo and continued by his successors, it was finished by the construction of the beautiful inner courtyard with two series of loggias, the work of G. F. Bergamini in 1665. In 1701 Alessandro Bergamini gave a uniform design to the façade by adding busts and balconies.

The Cathedral, whose façade is modern, dates from the 15th century and has subsequently been remodelled. The interior has a single nave which is flanked by chapels, the one underground serving as a pantheon for the princes and dukes of Massa.

The *Rocca* which towers above the town consists in the centre of a huge fortified *enceinte* with an innermost mediaeval part to which in the 15th and 16th centuries the Malaspina added a large Renaissance palace whose windows and cornices have a beautiful marble decoration. It was here that Eleanor of Este received Charles VIII. Other guests of the past include Catherine de Medici, Charles V, Pope Paul III and Michelangelo.

The road continues along the foot of hills covered with olive groves and passes below the ruins of the Aghinolfo Castle which was a powerful place in the 9th and 10th centuries.

We reach **PIETRASANTA**, which is dominated by the
12th-century Rocca di Sala. The town, founded in 1242 by
Guiscard Pietrasanta, Podestà of Lucca, was at that time
joined to the fortress by a line of crenellated walls which still
exist. The fortress withstood several sieges, notably those by
Charles VIII and Charles V.

Passing beneath the Porta Pisana with, on the left, the
ruins of Rocca Arrighini, we reach the lovely Piazza del
Duomo where we find the town's principal buildings, with
the red campanile of the Cathedral, the gilt façade of the
Church of S. Agostino which stands out against the hill, the
fountain, the clocktower and the Marzocco Column, all three
dating from the 16th century.

The Cathedral built in 1330 has a three-sectional façade,
which is decorated with a large rose-window by Lorenzo
Riccomanni, and three portals. The central one has, on the
tympanum, a *Crucifixion*, the one on the right a *Descent from
the Cross* and the one on the left a *Resurrection* by the Pisan
School. On the right of the central portal a *Saint John the
Baptist* by Stagio Stagi is framed by the coats-of-arms of the
House of Pietrasanta and the city of Florence. The isolated
campanile dates from the 15th and 16th centuries.

The interior has three naves which are separated by
columns. The two holy-water basins are youthful works of
Stagio Stagi and the marble pulpit is by Bastiano Bitozzi.

Adjacent to the Cathedral we find the 14th-century
Church of S. Agostino. It has a marble façade with three
large blind arcades and a series of elegant Gothic ones by
Riccomanno and Leonardo Riccomanni (1431).

The interior has a single nave with a timbered roof. On the
right there is a chapel with frescoes which portray the life of
Saint Augustine.

Continuing our tour of the *piazza*, we see the Palazzo
Pretorio with a gate of 1515. Taking Via Mazzini we reach
the Church of S. Biagio which has a fine 16th-century

cantor's tribune, a statue of a saint by Jacopo della Quercia and a *Virgin Enthroned* by Lorenzo Cellini. The 16th-century Church of S. Francesco has preserved its cloister with columns and its marble well by one of the Stagi.

Here we leave the N.1 which continues on to Viareggio, the most popular bathing resort on the Tyrrhenian coast, and Pisa, and take the road, on the left, to Lucca.

The road runs along the foot of hills covered with olive groves in the direction of Massarosa. Three kilometres away, to the north, at PIEVE A ELICI, we can see the beautiful Church of S. Pantaleone which was built in the first half of the 11th century and remodelled in the 13th. It has a graceful, pure façade and an elegant campanile. We then pass through Quiesa where a road, on the left, will lead us, three kilometres away to MASSACIUCCOLI, near the lake of the same name. Here we find the remains of a villa or Roman thermals known as the Bagno di Nerone dating from the 1st or 2nd century A.D. The ruined castle above the hill is partly Roman.

Five kilometres away, we can take the road on the right this time and after a kilometre and a half reach ARLIANO whose small church which is falling to pieces is considered the most ancient Romanesque construction in the region and probably dates from the 7th century. On the exterior, it is entirely flanked by large blind arcades and has a simple façade which is decorated with a sarcophagus. In the interior, there is a *Virgin and Child* by a 14th-century Pisan sculptor.

Close by, on the left, two kilometres away, we find the Carthusian Monastery of Farneta which was built in the early 14th century by two merchants of Lucca but enlarged and modified in the modern period. It has preserved a silver-gilt Byzantine reliquary of the 7th century.

Somewhat farther on, at Ponte S. Pietro, we are three kilometres from Nozzaro which is dominated by a picturesque 14th-century castle which stood opposite the Pisan fortifications of Ripafratta on the other side of the river. One of the towers has been made into the church steeple.

We soon reach LUCCA which is still surrounded by ramparts of rose-coloured stone against a background of greenery.

This charming city has numerous churches with luxurious façades and its narrow mediaeval streets are bordered by palaces.

After being a Roman colony and a *municipium*, Lucca under the Lombards became the seat of a powerful duchy. After the death of Countess Mathilda in 1119, it became a free city. In spite of continual struggles against its neighbours, the 12th and 13th centuries were a prosperous period for Lucca, thanks to the silk industry and to the banking activity of its merchants.

The struggles between Guelfs and Ghibellines affected its power and in 1314 the city fell into the hands of the tyrant Uguccione della Faggiola, the leader of the Tuscan Ghibellines and ruler of Pisa. Two years later Lucca regained her liberty and chose as captain-general Castruccio Castracani, who extended her domination over Pistoia, Volterra and Luni. On his death in 1328, Lucca passed into the hands of various suzerainties, but became independent again from 1400 to 1430 when the city was controlled by a wealthy merchant named Paolo Guinigi.

In 1805 Napoleon raised Lucca to a principality for the benefit of his sister Elisa and his brother-in-law Felice Baciocchi, thanks to whom the city enjoyed a new economic prosperity. In 1817 Lucca became a duchy and was wisely governed by Marie-Louise of Bourbon Parma.

The vast Piazza Napoleone, bordered by plane trees, stands in the centre of the city with the impressive Palazzo del Governo, the ancient Palazzo della Signoria, begun by Ammanati in 1578 and continued in 1728 by Francesco Pini in the same style. The palace was built on the site of the

Castraccio Castracani fortress which was torn down by the angry populace in 1368 and replaced by the Palazzo dei Guingi, which was ruined by the explosion of a powder-magazine.

The courtyard with its two storeys of arcades is impressive and leads to the Picture Gallery which contains remarkable works of art by Berlinghiero Berlinghieri, Deodato Orlandi, Fra Bartolomeo, Tintoretto, Canozzi da Landinara and others.

We then cross Piazza Puccini which communicates with Piazza S. Giovanni where we see the Church of S. Giovanni which consists of two buildings, a 12th-century church and a baptistery which was rebuilt in the 14th century. The church was re-done in 1622, but the façade flanked by pilasters has preserved its Romanesque portal framed by two columns surmounted by lions with its tympanum which has a small rose-window, its sculptured capitals and its frieze by Master Villano representing *The Virgin Between Archangels and Apostles*.

The interior has three naves separated by ancient columns, one of the capitals is Roman, the others Romanesque; it terminates in a transept and a deep semicircular apse. The coffer-ceiling is of 1589. A large arcade leads to the baptistery which is enclosed on three sides by blind arcades resting on clusters of columns which receive the thrust of the ribs of the cupola. In the centre there is an ancient baptismal vat which belonged to a Roman building.

The *piazza* in turn communicates with that of the Cathedral bordered, on the left, by the Palazzo Bernardi which was built by Ammanati in 1556. It is a pleasant sight with its embossed gates, its garden planted with trees which enclose it and, behind, the dome and crenellated campanile of the Church of S. Giovanni. On the other side, we find set against the impressive campanile of the Cathedral, also crenellated, the 13th-century Opera del Duomo with windows having three bays and, opposite, the façade of the

Cathedral. Rebuilt in 1060 by Bishop Anselmo da Baggio, who became Pope Alexander II, the Cathedral was remodelled in the early 13th century.

The façade, which has remained Romanesque, is built on to the campanile and fronted by a deep portico with three semicircular bays which are supported by pillars flanked by engaged columns topped by lions. The capitals have foliage decoration and one of them represents the genealogical tree of the Virgin. The upper part, which we owe to Master Guidetto da Como, has three storeys of blind arcades resting on elegant slender marble columns; there is great variety, some are smooth, others twisted.

Beneath the portico the wall of the façade, which is decorated with blind arcades and sculptures, has three wonderful portals. The sculptures between the portals, executed in 1233, are for the most part by an unknown master who was probably Lombard but influenced by the School of Pisa. The tympanum of the central portal is decorated with a *Christ in a Mandorla Supported by Two Angels* and the lintel with a *Madonna Between the Apostles*. The imposts of this portal and others are the work of Masseo Civitali, the nephew of the celebrated Matteo, and of Jacopo di Villa (1497).

On each side of the portal there are four bas-reliefs devoted to the life of Saint Martin and others to the Labours of the Months. Below, on the right, a medallion is a youthful work by Civitali.

The lintel of the right portal has a *Meeting of Saint Martin and the Arians* and the tympanum *The Beheading of Saint Regolo* which is one of Nicola Pisano's masterpieces. We are indebted to the same sculptor for *The Nativity* on the lintel of the left portal and for the very pathetic *Descent from the Cross* on the tympanum.

The lateral façades which are of a later date have blind arcades. On the lintel of one of the portals there is a *Pietà and Saints* from the workshop of Jacopo della Quercia.

Although the interior was transformed in the second half of the 14th century and beginning of the 15th, it has none the less a certain elegance. There are three high naves separated by pillars, a transept with two naves and a semicircular apse. Above the semicircular arcades of the central nave are the triple bays of the tribune topped by an oculus. The Gothic vaulting, whose ribs spring from pillars, has paintings with a blue background.

Attached to the inner wall of the façade is a wonderful group representing *Saint Martin Sharing his Cloak*, a copy of which exists on the exterior. This early 13th-century work shows a French influence.

In the right nave there is a wonderful panel by Ghirlandaio portraying *The Martyrdom of Saint Clement, The Entombment, The Martyrdom of Saint Sebastian* and *The Conversion of Saint Paul*. In the right transept we can see the tomb of Pietro da Noceto and that of Domenico Bertini which are both by Matteo Civitali. The following chapel, which has two lovely angels, is the work of Nicola and Vincenzo Civitali. Then in the next we find a wonderful monumental altar by Matteo Civitali (1484).

It is to the same artist that we owe the balustrade of the choir whose fine stained-glass windows are by Pandolo di Ugulino da Pisa (1485).

Then in the left transept we see the masterpiece of Fra Bartolomeo, *The Virgin and Child Between Saint Stephen and Saint John the Baptist*, a statue of *Saint John the Evangelist* by Jacopo della Quercia and above all the touching tomb of Ilaria del Caretto, the young wife of Paolo Guinigi, who died in 1405, with the figure prudently reclining in a carefully folded dress.

Finally in the left nave, the Templeto del Volto Santo is an elegant octagonal marble construction by Matteo Civitali. It contains an 11th- or 12th-century *Christ on the Cross* dressed in a tunic according to Byzantine iconography.

The Opera del Duomo, on the square alongside the Cathedral, has a remarkable collection of goldsmiths' work the principal pieces dating from the 15h century.

In visiting the churches of Lucca, we must start with that of S. Maria della Rosa. It was begun in 1309 but subsequently enlarged. The Renaissance door is by Matteo Civitali and the lateral façades are in the Pisan-Gothic style. In the 13th century the Church of S. Maria Forisportam stood beyond the walls of the city, the upper part dating from the 16th century. This is a building in the Pisan style decorated with blind arcades on the apse, the sides and the façade, which has two storeys. The three portals have richly decorated lintels and capitals. The tympanum on the left has a 12th-century *Virgin and Child* and the one on the right a 13th-century *Holy Bishop*.

The interior has three naves which are separated by columns and two pillars supporting high arcades whose capitals are partly Classical. The cupola was added in the 16th century when the central nave was given barrel-vaulting. The baptismal fonts are formed by a Palaeo-Christian sarcophagus which represents *Daniel in the Lions' Den*.

Continuing along Via S. Croce we reach the Gate of SS. Gervasio e Protasio which belonged to the ancient *enceinte*. Built in 1260, it is decorated with niches and flanked by two semicircular towers. Set against the gate, the Oratory of the Annunciation, a late 15th-century work is fronted by a portico.

If we wish to continue further, we will find in Via Elisa the Church of Santa Trinita of 1589 which contains one of the most charming works of Matteo Civitali, his *Madonna della Tosse*; and, opposite at No. 9, the Palazzo Buonvisi which was built in 1566 in the centre of a garden. Part of the decoration by the Salimbeni has been preserved.

We return to Via S. Croce which has some of the finest

palaces in Lucca: at No. 64, the 17th-century Palazzo
Mazzarosa with its collections of sculpture and works of art,
and the 16th-century Palazzo Bernardini with its ground-
floor decorated with embossed pilasters and its two storeys of
arched windows, the work of Nicolao Civitali. A courtyard is
bordered by a portico with columns and pilasters. On the
right of the square we can see the small 13th-century Church
of S. Benedetto, then taking a street on the right, the Church
of S. Giulia of the same period, with its graceful marble
façade.

Somewhat farther on, at the beginning of Via Fillungo,
one of the most lively and characteristic streets in the city,
we find the Church of S. Cristoforo which was rebuilt in the
13th century. The façade has five blind arcades which frame
three portals, the central one with a richly sculptured lintel.
A large rose-window above is of the late 14th century.
Opposite, the House of Monna Vanna (or Travaglio Tower)
dates from the 14th century. On the right of the church we
find the house of the artist Matteo Civitali whose works we
have just admired and, on the left, that of Giovanni Sercambi,
a 15th-century chronicler.

Then taking the short and crowded Via Roma we reach
the *piazza* which encloses the Church of S. Michele in Foro
which, after the Cathedral, is the most beautiful religious
building in Lucca and one of the most typical examples of
Pisan-Luccan architecture.

This is a 12th-century building which was gradually faced
with marble. The façade, lofty and greatly restored, is
entirely covered with blind arcades. Those below, high and
much wider, are surmounted by four further storeys, two
along the entire width of the façade, while the two above
decorate a gable. The design is both graceful and overloaded.
The whole is topped by a statue of *Saint Michael Destroying
the Dragon* between two angels. At one angle there is a fine
statue of *The Virgin and Child* by Civitali.

The lateral façades are likewise decorated with blind arcades, the large ones below continuing those of the front façade and being surmounted by a similar loggia which corresponds to that on the front façade. The campanile above the right transept is also decorated with small blind arcades.

The interior has three naves which are separated by columns with capitals of the period, except for several which are classic, and terminates in a transept and an apse. The timbered roof was replaced in the 16th century by vaulting.

In the transept we can admire a glazed terracotta by della Robbia which represents *The Virgin and Child* and in the left transept one of Filippino Lippi's finest works representing four saints.

Leaving Piazza S. Michele we take Via Caldera which leads to Piazza del Salvatore where we see the Veglio Tower and the 12th-century Church of S. Salvatore whose upper part was remodelled in the following century in the Gothic taste. The portals are decorated with beautiful sculptures by Biduino.

A street opposite enables us to see the grand 16th-century Palazzo Orsetti which is attributed to Nicolao Civitali and the 12th-century Church of S. Maria Corteorlandini which, although remodelled in the 18th century, has preserved its two lateral apses and, on the right side, a fine portal decorated with two lions.

The narrow Via del Moro, with its mediaeval houses and the 16th-century Palazzo del Municipio, and Via degli Asili with, at No. 33, the Palazzo Controni of 1667 and its curious flight of steps, lead us to the ancient 14th-century Church of S. Agostino whose campanile displays at its base vestiges of the ancient Roman theatre of the 2nd century.

We next take Via C. Battisti, bordered by 17th- and 18th-century palaces, which leads us to one of the most remarkable churches in Lucca, that of S. Frediano, whose massive

5. BARGA, PULPIT OF THE
CATHEDRAL.

crenellated campanile rises before us. It was built from 1112
to 1147 and remodelled in the 13th century on the site of an
8th-century basilica. The façade, which is flanked by pilasters,
has three plainly decorated portals, while the central part,
above a gallery with slender columns topped by an architrave, has a large mosaic by Berlinghiero Berlinghieri
representing *The Ascension*.

The interior, which is on a basilican plan, has three naves
separated by columns with antique capitals and terminates
in a large apse which was rebuilt when the orientation of the
church was reversed. In the 14th century, chapels were
added to the sides.

At the entrance to the right nave, the lustral font is a
remarkable 12th-century aedicule which rises out of a
circular bowl. It is decorated on the exterior by bas-reliefs,
one section representing scenes from *The Life of Moses* by a
certain Master Roberto, while the others, *The Good Shepherd*
and *The Apostles*, are executed in a less refined manner.
The aedicule and its cover are decorated with other sculptures in the style of Biduino.

In the left nave, in the fourth chapel, there is a graceful
Gothic marble polyptych by Jacopo della Quercia with,
beneath the canopy, the statues of *The Virgin and Four Saints*
while the predella has subtle and vigorous scenes. In front,
the tombstones of Lorenzo Trenta and his wife by the same
artist are equally striking. On the altar there is a fine
painting by Francesco Francia. The semicircular apse is
surmounted by a loggia.

Then we go out into Via Fillungo leading to the market
square which occupies the site of the ancient Roman
amphitheatre.

We next find the Palazzo Brancoli with its fine portal and
its loggia and, opposite, the Palazzo Buonvisi, then the
Portone dei Borghi which was part of the ancient *enceinte*
of 1260.

The 12th-century Church of S. Pietro Somaldi manifests its beautiful façade of grey and white stone of 1248. It has three portals in the Pisan style, two twin windows and is decorated with two rows of blind arcades. The church is flanked by a massive campanile. The central portal is decorated with two lions and a bas-relief by Guido da Coma portraying *Jesus Presenting the Keys to Saint Peter* (1203).

The Church of S. Francesco was built in 1228 and remodelled in the 14th and 17th centuries. The façade has a semicircular portal between two large blind arcades, also a rose-window. On each side of the Gothic portal there are two tombs each surmounted by an aedicule.

The interior has a single nave and a timbered roof. In a chapel on the right of the tribune, there are beautiful frescoes by the 15th-century Florentine School. The cloister alongside contains several tombs.

We can see also, on the left, the ancient Oratory of S. Franceschetto of 1309 and the Casa Fondora where Dante was the guest of Gentucca, and then take Via della Quarquonia which leads us to the Villa di Paolo Guinigi, an impressive brick construction built in 1418 by the princes of Lucca. A gallery with semicircular arcades is surmounted by elegant trilobulate triple bays. An interesting museum of sculpture and painting has recently been installed there.

Retracing our steps in order to reach Via Guinigi, we find, at the beginning, the small 13th-century Church of SS. Simone e Giuda, with its simple façade of grey and white stone. In the interior there is a fine statue by Francesco di Valdambrino. Somewhat farther on, we discover the remains of the Casa dei Guinigi, a 14th-century brick palace with a crenellated tower, a portico now walled-up and beautiful trilobulate windows which are either twin or associated by threes or fours.

Opposite, another palace, which is richer and more

elegant, dates from the second half of the 14th century. The ground floor was remodelled in the 16th century and the two upper storeys of brick have fine windows with four bays. Finally, on the corner of Via S. Andrea, the Loggia dei Guinigi is a curious example of a mediaeval loggia.

We will return to the centre of the city along Via S. Andrea which enables us to see, in the second street on the left, the small 12th- and 14th-century Church of S. Anastasia which is built of brick with marble bands. The façade is decorated with majolica bowls and has three twin windows and a marble portal of 1167; the apse is charming.

Farther on, on the left, the 13th-century Church of S. Andrea has a fine portal surmounted by two lions. Opposite, is the 14th-century Casa Caselli.

We leave, on Piazza Giudicciono, the Palazzo of the same name which was built by Civitali in the 16th century, and enter Via Fillungo where we find the 13th-century clock tower which faces another tower of the 14th century and a brick house with twin windows.

Taking Via Cenani, where we see the early 16th-century Palazzo Cenani which is attributed to Nicolao Civitali, we reach the 12th-century Church of S. Giusto with its pleasant façade decorated above with two galleries of blind arcades and having three portals. The lateral ones are in the early Pisan style, the central one, much richer, is typical of the Luccan style with its lions and its crowded lintel. Opposite, the early 16th-century Palazzo Gigli is attributed to Matteo and Nicolao Civitali.

After having crossed Piazza Napoleone we reach the early Romanesque Church of S. Alessandro which was rebuilt about 1150 and completed on the apse side in the 13th century by a decoration of blind arcades. The restrained marble façade with white and grey bands has a classic portal with pediment and a high 13th-century bas-relief representing *Pope Alexander*. On the right side, a portal with a porch supported by consoles by Stagio Stagi has, on the tympanum, a *Virgin* by Consani.

The Dominican Church of S. Romano was rebuilt in 1280 and enlarged on the side of the apse in 1373. In the interior we can admire the handsome tomb of Saint Romano with a *Pietà* and the recumbent statue of the saint by Matteo Civitali.

Finally, there is the Church of S. Paolino which was begun by Baccio da Montelupo in 1522 and finished by Bastiano Bortolani in 1539 on the site of a Roman edifice. The Renaissance façade has three series of pilasters and the interior, with its single nave, transept and communicating chapels, is decorated with two series of pilasters. In the choir, we can see the Paleo-Christian sarcophagus which is decorated with *The Good Shepherd* and contains the body of the saint. The stalls are by Salimbene Magni.

In Via Galli Tassi the 17th-century Palazzo Mansi has a fine loggia on the first storey. In the interior, the luxurious apartments have preserved their decoration and furnishings.

We will end this visit of Lucca with a tour of the city ramparts which were built from 1504 to 1645. They are equipped with demi-lunes, bastions and a platform. This wonderful promenade bordered with trees offers, on one side, a fine view of the city and, on the other, that of the neighbouring countryside.

Several of the gates are architectually interesting, notably the Porta S. Pietro.

In the surroundings of Lucca there are many splendid villas. Before heading for S. Miniato, we will make a detour in the direction of the hills where these villas are clustered.

We leave by way of the N.12 towards Bagni di Lucca, where Montaigne took a cure which he has discussed at length, and ascend the valley of the Serchio. But at the end of seven kilometres, at Fraga, we will take a road on the right which leads to MARLIA where we will visit the Villa Marlia (or Orsetti) also known as the Imperial Villa, for it was the summer residence of Elisa Bacciochi. In the 14th century, the country belonged to the Orsetti who were called the "Paladins of Marlia", because Stefano Orsetti had brought back a trophy in the shape of a tail from a pasha's horse.

The castle, which was made into a villa in the 16th century by the Orsetti, was in the 18th century surrounded by magnificent gardens with tree-lined halls with walls of trimmed green oaks set around a huge artificial lake. A circular *salon* with a fountain led to a delightful theatre amongst the trees, which was enlivened by Harlequins and Columbines.

Orsetti family being extinct, Elisa Bonaparte acquired the castle at the close of the 18th century and commissioned Bienaimé and Lazzarini to enlarge the villa and the gardens. She decorated the villa in the Empire Style with frescoes by Prudhon and Tosanelli, and laid out a huge park in the English style. In front of the villa there was a long lawn of grass which ran down to a lake.

In 1820 Marie-Louise built an observatory in the form of a "Temple of Urania", flanked by a library and a study, and a casino which was used as a ballroom. Its former guests include the great violinist Paganini, who gave several concerts there, and Metternich.

At SEGROMINGNO we will see another outstanding villa, the Villa Mansi, which we are allowed to visit. It was built in the 17th century for the Mansi family and about 1742 was transformed according to the design by Filippo Juvara. We must complete our visit to Lucca with the Palazzo Mansi and its famous bedroom. In the 17th century the villa was the summer home of Lucida Mansi, the merry widow whose amorous adventures have become legendary. She is said to have retained her extraordinary beauty for 30 years, thanks to a pact with the Devil; each day she had to bathe in the

artificial lake in the garden. One night she was struck dead
by lightning, but her ghost, it is said, still haunts the lake.

Juvara's Baroque façade is charming. Although the garden
has been partly transformed into the English style, the
artificial lake still exists with its balustrades and statues.
The interior has preserved its Empire furnishings.

In order to regain the road from Montecatini to Borgonuovo, we pass through CAMIGLIANO S. GEMMA where
we can see the luxurious Villa Torriginani which was built in
the 17th century for the Santini family. In the 18th century it
was owned by the Torrigiani. We enter through a wonderful
avenue of cypress trees. The Baroque façade is very graceful
with its loggias, its three storeys of balustrades and its
statues. The part facing the garden was transformed into the
English style in the 18th century, but the two irregular
artificial lakes on either side of the villa have been preserved. Behind, the 18th-century garden has been respected.
We can see the small secret garden of Flora with its disconcerting sprays of water, which are the most elaborate in
all Italy. The alarmed visitor takes cover beneath the roof
of the Temple of Flora where he receives a final shower from
the cornucopia and the goddess's wrought-iron crown of
flowers.

At Borgonuovo we take the road on the left to Pescia, but
at Lappato, we will go to see, two kilometres away, at
S. GENNARO, a beautiful Romanesque church whose façade
and left side are well preserved. The interior, which has three
naves separated by columns with wonderful capitals, contains a fine ambo of 1162 by Master Filippo, decorated with
symbols of the Evangelists. In addition, there is a polychrome
terracotta *Herald Angel* by the School of Verrocchio and
several 15th-century *Virgins*.

We return to the road and at Ponte all' Abate take the one
to COLLODI which is but a kilometre away. On the right, at
the foot of a hill clothed with rich vegetation, is the Villa

Garzoni, whose garden is one of the most extraordinary in Italy. A visit can be paid. Part of the reason for doing this is that the garden lies in a high position near a mediaeval castle which was made into a villa. In the 15th century the Castle of Collodi belonged to the Republic of Lucca. It was subsequently purchased by the Garzoni family who laid out the garden in 1625. The villa itself was developed in the 18th century. From the windows we can see an *ensemble* of flower-beds, artificial lakes and fountains all pleasantly arranged. In addition to a large cascade, we can still see, in the centre of the highest terrace, an artificial lake which is surmounted by a huge statue of *Fame* between others which personify the cities of Florence and Lucca. In the 18th century, Ottaviano Diodati arranged delightful baths, a stage for an orchestra, a woodland theatre, curious terracotta seats in the form of sea-shells and troupes of monkeys playing at ball.

Collodi is the birthplace of the author of *Pinocchio*. We can see the curious monument which is devoted to him; and the church which has several interesting paintings. Then we continue as far as VILLA BASILICA where the late 12th-century Piscan-Luccan Romanesque church with three naves is flanked by a much older campanile. The apse is decorated with elegant blind arcades and in the interior there is a *Crucifixion* by Berlinghiero Berlinghieri. The 11th-century crypt is that of an earlier building.

We will return to Ponte all' Abate. We can see, on the right, a kilometre after Alberghi, the small, very pure Romanesque Church of S. Piero in Campo, its façade decorated with blind arcades and its handsome capitals.

PESCIA is a town which was important during the time of the Medici. There are several churches, the most interesting being the late 13th-century S. Francesco with a façade refurbished in 1505 and remodelled in 1632. In the interior we can admire one of Bonaventura Berlinghieri's masterpieces, a painting portraying *Saint Francis and Six Scenes from his Life*.

It was executed in 1235, only nine years after the Saint's death.

The Cathedral, which was rebuilt by Antonio Ferri in 1693, has a modern façade and a massive campanile of 1306.

If we have time, we can ascend the valley which opens on to Pescia in order to see, 12 kilometres away, near Castelvecchio, the isolated Church of S. Ansano. This is a Romanesque edifice with a three-sectional façade flanked by blind arcades in its lower part and, above, by blind arcades which are supported by historiated consoles. Alongside the apse is a massive campanile. The nave is separated from the side-aisles by massive columns and the choir is above the crypt, which has four naves.

Two kilometres away from Pescia we can see the Church of UZZANO. It has a single nave which dates from the 13th century. The attractive façade has a curious gable which is decorated with blind arcades.

We have the choice of continuing to Montecatini Terme, one of Italy's largest and most popular spas, and at Pistoia join Itinerary III, or follow this present one which at Altopascio rejoins the road from Lucca to Florence by way of Empoli.

Before reaching Altopascio, however, we will proceed as far as Borgo a Buggiano, then ascend to BUGGIANO CASTELLO, a small town which seems to be falling apart. We enter beneath the Porta S. Martino to find ourselves confronted with a picturesque *piazza* dominated by a tower and enclosed by ancient buildings, including the Palazzo Pretorio, a solid 12th-century building decorated with coats-of-arms, and the *Pieve*, the Romanesque church of a Benedictine abbey founded in 1038 and partly rebuilt at a later date. The portal is decorated with two lions.

The interior has three naves which are separated by columns with antique capitals and, on the left, by pillars. The baptistery adjacent to the façade was part of a 12th-century ambo.

We will continue to ALTOPASCIO which in the Middle Ages was the seat of the Knights Hospitalers of the Order of Altopascio. Founded about the middle of the 11th century and suppressed in 1459, a hospice for pilgrims was added in 1084. The Church of S. Jacopo Maggiore has preserved part of the Romanesque building with a typically Luccan façade whose upper part is polychrome with a high-relief of *Saint James* by Biduino and a gable decorated with blind arcades, as at Uzzano. The crenellated stone campanile of 1280, which is the finest one in the region, has a bell of 1327 known as "The Strayed One" which rang for those who had lost their way in the Cerbaie woods or the Bientina marshes.

The road crosses the Cerbaie hills, then the Fucecchio marshes and we finally reach FUCECCHIO which in the early 11th century was the fief of the powerful Lombard family of the Counts Cadolingi di Borgo Nuovo, who held their court there.

On the summit of the hill overlooking the town stands the fortress that was built by the Florentines in 1323; in a cypress wood we can find the remains of curtain walls and several towers.

One of the most interesting churches is the collegiate one of S. Giovanni Battista which, although built in the 10th century, was completely transformed in the 18th. Equally interesting is the Church of S. Salvatore which belonged to an abbey founded in 986 by Countess Gemma, the daughter of Landolfo, Prince of Benevento. Fronted by a gallery and dominated by a high, crenellated, 13th-century tower, it has a single nave with a timbered roof.

There are several palaces in Via Donateschi and in Via Castruccio, also in Piazza Montanelli and Piazza Vittorio Veneto.

S. MINIATO is a town which deserves a careful visit, for it has preserved a certain character and several churches are quite interesting. The most remarkable is the Church of

S. Domenico on Piazza del Popolo. It was rebuilt in 1330 and has a rough façade and a large portal.

The interior has a single nave with side-chapels and was remodelled in the 17th century. There are several outstanding works of art, notably, on the other side of the façade, a *Saint Catherine of Alexandria* and a *Saint Michael* by Rossello di Jocopo Franchi and, in the chapel on the right of the choir, the tomb of Giovanni Chellini, a Florentine doctor who died in 1461, which may be the work of Donato Benti.

Several rooms and corridors of the monastery are decorated with 14th-century frescoes. The ancient cloister is now used for municipal purposes.

An arcade leads from Piazza del Popolo to Piazza della Repubblica where we see the Seminary, whose upper part is decorated with geometrical designs and medallions by Luigi Cigoli, and the Bishop's Palace, the ancient 13th-century Imperial Palace where Countess Mathilda was born in 1046. In 1077 she made a gift of all her vast possessions to the Church. It was at her castle of Canossa that the Emperor Henry IV did penance to Pope Gregory VII, better known as Hildebrand.

Three flights of steps lead to the Prato del Duomo with its fine view over the plain of the Arno and the distant Apennines. The Cathedral was built in the 12th century but subsequently remodelled. The Romanesque brick façade, whose upper part is well preserved, has three 16th-century portals and is decorated with 13th-century majolica coats-of-arms. The massive campanile is a tower of the ancient castle and still equipped with machicolation.

The interior, which is in the form of a Latin cross, has three naves which are separated by columns.

Of the fortress of Frederick II there remains merely a tower in which Pier della Vigna, slandered by the courtiers, was imprisoned and branded in 1249.

Of interest also are the Municipio, the Church of S.

Francesco which was rebuilt in 1276 and enlarged in the
15th century, and at No. 4, Via P. Maioli, the Palazzo
Buonaparte where Napoleon stayed in 1797 when he visited
his relative, the Canon Filippo Buonaparte. Via P. Maioli
and Via IV Novembre have several 16th-century palaces
with embossed gates and windows.

If we have time we can visit the Instituto Magistrale which
has a museum devoted to the works of Luigi Cigoli; there is
also a *Crucifixion* by Deodato Orlandi of 1301.

Let us continue to Empoli, but a kilometre before that
place, we will stop in order to see the Church of S. Maria a
Ripa which is fronted by a portico. It contains several
interesting works of art, notably a polychrome terracotta
Santa Lucia by Andrea della Robbia.

EMPOLI is a lively and picturesque town with, on the
main square which is surrounded by porticos, the beautiful
façade of the Collegiate Church which was rebuilt in 1093 in
the Florentine Romanesque style of S. Miniato al Monte at
Florence, but in the 18th century the interior was dressed up
in the Baroque style.

The façade, which is faced with white and green marble,
has preserved five blind arcades in the lower part, but the
upper part, square and terminating in a tympanum, dates
from 1736.

Some outstanding works of art can be seen in the museum
of the Collegiate Church which is installed in the baptistery
and various other rooms. In the baptistery there are magnificent paintings by Masolino, Pontormo, Bicci di Lorenzo,
Lorenzo Monaco, Filippino Lippi, Botticini, baptismal fonts
by the School of Donatello, sculptures by Mino da Fiesole,
Tino di Camaino, various other works of art, including an
Eternal Father by Andrea della Robbia.

We can also visit the 14th-century Church of S. Stefano
which has three naves separated by large tierspoint arcades
and a timbered vaulting. Above the door leading to the

sacristy there are beautiful frescoes by Masolino da Panicale, notably a *Virgin and Child Between two Angels*.

We then pass through PONTORME, the birthplace of the painter Jacopo da Carrucci, better known as Il Pontormo. We can see the Church of S. Michele and, some distance from the houses, the Church of S. Martino whose semi-circular Romanesque apse has a fine *Virgin and Child* by Michele da Firenze.

We reach MONTELUPO FIORENTINO at the junction of the Pesa and the Arno. The Church of S. Giovanni Evangelista, which was built in the 18th century, has a *Virgin and Child Between Several Saints* by the workshop of Botticelli.

We can see also the ruins of the ancient castle which was built by the Florentines and, beyond the Pesa, taking an avenue of plane trees, the villa of the Medici known as l'Ambrogiana. Square in plan with four angle towers, it was built by Ferdinand I from the design by Bernardo Buontalenti. It is now a mental hospital.

We leave, on the right, the Villa Antinori, which was once the stronghold of the Strozzi family, pass through Camaioni and follow the banks of the Arno which makes several bends. Leaving Signa, on the other side of the river, we soon reach FLORENCE which is all too well-known for me to describe.

ITINERARY III

FROM LA SPEZIA, MODENA AND BOLOGNA
TO FLORENCE BY WAY OF PISTOIA

1. FROM LA SPEZIA TO FLORENCE

*Aulla — Castelnuovo — Barga — Loppia — Coreglia —
Borgo — Diecimo — Bagni di Lucca — S. Cassiano —
S. Marcello — Pistoia — Prato — Poggio a Caiano —
Signa.*

THIS itinerary is a variation of the preceding one.
It will enable those who already know the coastal
road to reach Lucca and Pistoia by way of the
mountains. It is not a rapid road, but, although it offers no
great archaeological curiosities, it will introduce us to
several interesting churches.

We take the N.62 which ascends the valley of the Magra
and leads us to AULLA, a commercial town which owes its
origin to the Abbey of S. Caprasio founded in 884. Of the
ancient abbatial church there remains merely the apse which
moreover has been remodelled. In 1543 the Genoese patri-
cian, Adamo Centurione, bought the abbey and the Castle
of Malaspina and built the Brunella, a rectangular fort,
reinforced at each angle by a bastion, overlooking the valley.
It still exists.

We leave the valley of the Magra for that of the Aulella
and take the N.63 which passes through Gassano. Then taking the road to Reggio, eight kilometres away after the small

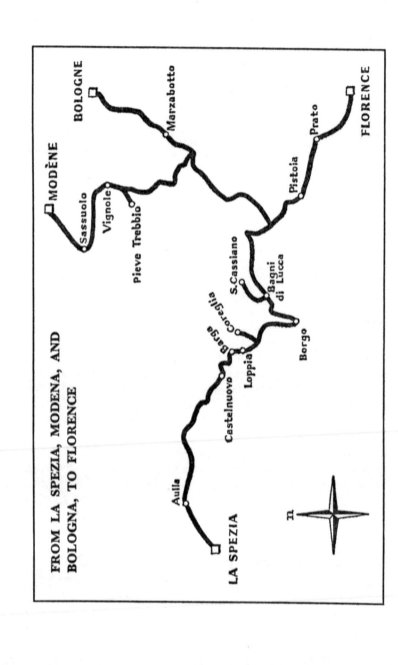

FROM LA SPEZIA, MODENA, AND BOLOGNA, TO FLORENCE

town of Fivizzano, we can see the 13th-century PIEVE DI S. PAOLO DI VENDASO, a basilican church with three naves whose apse is decorated with Lombard blind arcades and whose capitals, although primitive, are quite fascinating. The very simple façade has an attractive twin window above a semicircular portal.

We then pass through CASOLA IN LUNIGIANA, which has preserved numerous 15th- and 16th-century houses and the remains of its ramparts. On the *piazza* we can see an isolated, massive cylindrical tower and, somewhat apart, the Pieve di Codiponte, a late Romanesque structure with three naves which are separated by columns with sculptured capitals.

The road becomes uneven and, rapidly ascending among chestnut trees, reaches the slope of the Lunigiana. It then passes through the Colle di Carpinelli at an altitude of 2,600 feet and reaches the valley of the Serchio.

We arrive at CASTELNUOVO DI GARFAGNANA where we see the ancient fortress which dates from the 12th century. Built on an irregular plan, it consists of a massive, square, central tower and small towers on the south-east with a loggia. The poets Ariosto and Testi stayed here.

We continue to descend the narrow and winding valley of the Serchio and, at the end of 10 kilometres, take the road to BARGA.

This town, with its ancient quarters on the summit of the hill, is not lacking in character in spite of the damage caused during the last war. The Cathedral, which stands on the highest part and dominates the town, consists of an 11th-century building which was enlarged in the 12th century. Fronted by a narrow terrace, the Lombard Romanesque façade is decorated with two rows of blind arcades supported by historiated consoles. The handsome portal is flanked by two columns which are surmounted by lions with, on the lintel, a bas-relief representing grape gathering. On the left side, flanked by a massive, crenellated tower likewise decorated with blind arcades, we see a second portal whose sculptures devoted to two feasts are in the style of Biduino.

The interior, which has three naves separated by pillars and a timbered roof, contains a wonderful pulpit by marble-workers of the School of Guidetto; it is one of the best preserved of the School of Lucca of the second half of the 12th century before Nicola Pisano. It stands on four columns of pink marble, the two in front resting on lions and one behind on the back of a bearded old man. Bas-reliefs represent *The Adoration of the Magi, The Nativity, The Annunciation* and *The Prophet Isaiah*.

In the choir we can admire a polychrome marble screen and a beautiful *Saint Christopher*, a 12th-century work of polychrome wood. The treasure chamber has beautiful pieces, notably chalices and 14th- and 15th-century crosses.

We can see also the Palazzo Pretorio with the 14th-century loggia of the Podestà and on the *piazza comunale* the 16th-century Palazzo Comunale and the Market Loggia of the same period.

The road which takes us directly to Fornace passes through LOPPIA. Immediately before reaching the village we see the Pieve S. Maria which dates from the 10th century, but was rebuilt in the 13th in the Pisan style, that is, the façade decorated with semicircular blind arcades. The rest of the gable has a row of small blind arcades. The campanile has three storeys of twin windows.

The interior has three naves and contains 14th-century polychrome statues.

After returning to the valley, we can again ascend as far as COREGLIA ANTELMINELLI, a picturesque town lying on a hill planted with chestnut trees, with the 13th-century Church of S. Michele flanked by a massive tower.

Our principal road continues to descend the Serchio and before reaching Bagni di Lucca, we can see BORDO A

PIEVE TREBBIO, CHURCH OF S.
GIOVANNI BATISTA.

8. PISTOIA, CATHEDRA

MOZZANO, whose Church of S. Jacopo has a remarkable group of 15th- and 16th-century sculptures, then DIECIMO, where we will find the isolated Church of S. Maria. This is a severe, simple late 12th-century building. The façade has a semicircular portal, with a fine sculptured lintel, and a twin window. On the right is a splendid crenellated campanile in the Luccan style decorated with blind arcades and having twin, double, triple and quadruple bays.

The harmonious interior has three naves which are separated by square pillars with bands of green stone. We can see the remains of an ambo and various sculptures.

We will then ascend to BAGNI DI LUCCA, a charming spa which Montaigne visited. Its sulphate-sodium-calcium waters did him much good. In his *Voyage en Italie* he describes in great detail not only his cure but also the pleasant company he had.

The spa, which stands on the summit of a wooded hill, has preserved a certain character. It was popular in the early 19th century and among its visitors were Byron, Shelley, Heine and Carducci.

A road leads to the parish church of SAN CASSIANO DI CONTRONE whose fine 13th-century façade is flanked by a high crenellated tower of an earlier date. The façade is decorated on three storeys with blind arcades which are resting on slender columns. Below a twin window there is a wonderful portal whose tympanum, arch mouldings and lintel have curious human figures, fantastic animals and interlacing designs treated in a barbaric and powerful manner, inspired by Pre-Romanesque art.

In the sacristy we can see a 15th-century equestrian group in the manner of Jacopo della Quercia and a 15th-century *Annunciation* in the Pisan style.

The road follows the winding, picturesque valley of the Lima and reaches POPIGLIO which is dominated by a high tower. The 12th- and 13th-century Church of S. Maria

Assunta has a simple façade which is flanked by a campanile. In the interior, there is a pulpit decorated with 13th-century Pisan bas-reliefs.

We next reach S. MARCELLO PISTOIESE whose Romanesque church had its interior remodelled in 1610, then we return to the road which follows the valley of the Reno, the N.66, and descend to Pistoia.

We now trace the itinerary from Módena and a few pages further on I will describe the remainder of the distance to Florence.

2. FROM MÓDENA AND BOLOGNA TO FLORENCE

Sassuolo — Spilamberto — Vignola — Pieve Trebbio — Marzabotto — Pistoia — Prato — Poggio a Caiano — Signa.

The road from Bologna to Pistoia, which I shall describe a few pages further on, is not very interesting from the archaeological point of view, and so for those who are already familiar with Bologna I propose a road from Módena which will introduce them to several little-known buildings.

We head for SASSUOLO, a town which long belonged to the House of Este. Transformed in the 15th century by Borso d'Este, the Castle was rebuilt in 1634 by Bartolomeo Avanzini for Francesco I. It is now a military academy, but a visit can be authorised.

Let us enter the interior which has preserved its splendid decoration, the colossal groups at the entrance, the Fountain of Neptune by Raggi which stands in the courtyard, the statues which decorate the Staircase of Honour and, above all, the stucco work and the frescoes of the stately suites.

We can admire, notably, the *salon* of Fortune, the walls painted by Galluzi and the vaulting by Jean Boulanger, the Chamber of Love decorated by Rosa and Boulanger, the

Chamber of the Virtues of the Este and the Chamber of Genius by the same artists and, above all, the Gallery with frescoes by Boulanger and his assistants, Monti, Baldassare Bianchi and Cittadini. The walls have animated landscape scenes, and the elliptical vaulting likewise is covered with frescoes.

Opposite the park, which for the most part has disappeared, the Casino of the Belvedere, now private property, is decorated with *The Twelve Pleasure Resorts of the House of Este*.

FIORANO MODENESE is dominated by a green hill where once stood a castle which was destroyed in 1510. The Santa della Madonna of 1634, but finished in the 19th century, offers little interest. We will travel to Maranello in order to reach SPILAMBERTO, lying the centre of a fertile agricultural region. The fortress, which was rebuilt over the ruins of an early castle, is still quite picturesque. Opposite, is the well-preserved, massive Torrione Tower which dates from the 13th century.

The Church of S. Adriano, which was built in 1210 but remodelled at a later date, has a painting by Zoboli and the Church of S. Giovanni an 11th-century bronze Crucifix.

VIGNOLA is famous, not only for its cherries, but also for its fortress which was built in the 14th and 15th centuries and in 1577 passed into the hands of Jacopo Buoncompagni.

Much of the work is done by Giacomo Barozzi (1507–1573), one of the greatest architects of the Renaissance, known as Il Vignola, who was born here. The fortress is flanked by four high square towers which, like the entrance towers, are surmounted by oblong machicolation peculiar to military buildings of the region.

We can visit the courtyard, which is dominated by the lofty Nonantola Tower, and several rooms which have preserved their frescoes with motifs of coats-of-arms, emblems and birds. Those of the chapel date from the 15th century and are devoted to religious subjects. We can follow the watch path as well.

On Piazza Cavour facing the fortress we find the 16th- and 17th-century Palazzo Buoncompagni with an embossed portal and in the interior a famous oval staircase by Vignola with suspended steps.

A good meal can be had at the Ristorante Florita.

We will now follow the valley of the Panaro and soon discover GUIGLIA spread out on its hill. The town has preserved merely a quadrangular tower incorporated into an 18th-century *château*, now made into a hotel, surrounded by gardens. This tower is all that remains of a 14th-century castle which belonged to the Bolognese, then to the House of Este.

Farther on, at La Tagliata, we will take the road which after a kilometre and a half leads us to PIEVE TREBBIO, a village situated in sight of the Sassi della Rocca, a huge collection of monolithic needles formed by erosion, the highest measuring 225 feet.

In the centre of its highest part there are two caves in which early Christians sought refuge. Later when Europe was overrun by the Huns, these same caves were used as places of safety.

Opposite the village, a lane of pine and cypress trees leads to the Romanesque Church of S. Giovanni Battista which dates from the 9th or 10th century. The façade has a single portal surmounted by a sarcophagus decorated with sculptures, and a twin window. On the left side there rises a massive campanile which is isolated from the rest of the church.

The interior in the basilican plan has three naves separated by pillars with engaged columns and fine capitals supporting semicircular arcades. There are three apses, the central one containing a ciborium which is resting on four slender columns. The choir is fronted by an ambo and beautiful sculptured screens with, below, a crypt having very slender columns.

Opposite the church, the small baptistery contains a baptismal font for immersion which probably dates from the 9th century.

We then travel through Rocca Malatina and a forest of chestnut trees, then Zocca and, after a picturesque but uneven series of hills, we will return to the N.64 from Bologna.

*

*   *

After the Mausoleum of Marconi, built in 1941 below the villa where he made his first experiments in radio transmission, the N.64 passes through MARZABOTTO where the remains of an Etruscan town of the 6th century B.C. have been discovered. It was destroyed by the Gauls about the middle of the 4th century.

The archaeological zone lies some 500 yards from the town. We enter along Via Porrettana and find a museum which contains objects discovered during excavation.

Outside, we can see the citadel with the remains of two sacred buildings with triple *cella* which were dedicated to a heavenly triad and to an earthly one with their corresponding altars. In the centre of the smaller one there is a well which symbolised the path to the Underworld. The larger building is one of the most remarkable Etruscan monuments in existence. In addition, there are the ruins of another temple and beneath the citadel a fountain with its canalisations.

The original design of the town is preserved with its eight quarters delimited by a rectangular street running north and south to which transversal streets running east and west have been added. The main street is astonishingly wide. The roadway and lateral kerbs are 15 feet each. Narrower streets run parallel to the others.

Thus, as early as the 6th century B.C., the Tyrrhenians had modern towns with square houses built of stone, the rooms being grouped around an atrium with, in the centre, an *impluvium* which collected rainwater, thanks to a *compluvium* (an opening in the roof). Near the atrium was the kitchen, also used as the dining-room, with a hearth and a water tap.

There are two necropoli, the one to the east reached by the *decumanus maximus*, the other to the west, near a small artificial lake.

We cross the large fertile valley, leaving an attractive Renaissance church on the left and pass through Vergato, which suffered greatly during the last war, then through Poretta Terme, an important watering place.

After Ponte della Venturina we enter Tuscany and continue to follow the valley, now narrow and wooded, before descending towards the pleasant hills dotted with cypress trees which surround Pistoia and create a serene picture of the Tuscan landscape.

PISTOIA is the very image of those Italian towns which were torn by factions during the Middle Ages. Unable to decide between Pope and Emperor, they were in turn Guelf and Ghibelline, siding with the Whites or the Blacks in order to preserve, above all, their independence. The worst moments for Pistoia occurred in 1305 when, after being besieged by Florence and Lucca for 11 months, the town decided to surrender. The ramparts were dismantled and the women sold as slaves, but the town regained its strength and in 1314 withstood the assault of Uguccione della Faggiola, Prince of Lucca.

In spite of the recent destruction caused by American bombers who wiped out the Church of S. Giovanni Battista, Pistoia has a number of splendid mediaeval and Renaissance monuments. Piazza del Duomo, with the Cathedral, the Baptistery and the Palazza Pretario, is one of the most attractive squares in all Italy.

The Cathedral, which dates from the 5th century but was rebuilt in the 12th and 13th centuries in the Pisan Romanesque style, has a fine façade fronted by a portico, added in 1311, resting on elegant columns. The central arcade, much higher, is the opening of a coffer vaulting of glazed terracotta, an exquisite work by Andrea della Robbia to whom we are also indebted for one of his masterpieces, *The Virgin and Child between Two Angels* (1505), on the tympanum of the central portal.

Above the portico, the central part has three storeys of loggias and the gable is framed by two statues, the one by Jacopo di Mazzeo, the other by Andrea Vacca. On the left, the steeple, which in its lower part is a massive Lombard tower, was transformed in the 13th century by the addition of three storeys of elegant loggias in the Pisan style built of white and green marble, topped by a 16th-century cupola.

The interior of three naves is of majestic simplicity with its central nave having timbered vaulting and its columns with varied capitals. In the right nave, we can see the tomb of Cino da Pistoia, a Gothic aedicule surmounted by a tabernacle, and the Chapel of S. Jacopo with its silver altar weighing more than two hundred weight, one of the masterpieces of Italian goldsmith art. The first part was executed in 1287 and the rest at various times by different artists.

Our ticket allows us also to visit the diocesan museum which is installed in the sacristy, and consists notably of 14th-century chalices and reliquaries.

In the chapel on the left of the choir, we can admire *The Virgin Between Saint Zeno and Saint John the Baptist*. This work was begun by Verrocchio but finished by his pupil Lorenzo di Credi; it is considered the latter's masterpiece. In the same chapel there is a stele with a high-relief figure of Bishop Donato de Medici, who founded the chapel. The work was executed in 1475 by either Rossellino or Verrocchio.

Finally in the left nave, the monument of Cardinal Niccola Forteguerri has two statues, *Hope* and *Faith*, which are probably by Verrocchio, while the *Christ and the Angels* is very likely the work of Lorenzo di Credi. *Charity* is by Lorenzetto. At the entrance to the church, the baptismal fonts are by Andrea Ferrucci da Fiesole from the design by Benedetto da Majano.

Opposite the Cathedral is the baptistery which was begun in 1338 by Cellino di Nese from the design by Andrea Pisano. This elegant Gothic edifice is octagonal in shape, faced with white and green marble with, between the three portals, a blind gallery. The principal door has finely sculptured capitals, scenes from *The Life of Saint John the Baptist* on the architrave and, on the tympanum, a *Virgin and Child* which is probably by Tommaso and Nino da Pontedera, the sons and pupils of Andrea da Pontedera.

On the right the Palazzo Pretorio is a severe construction of 1367 which was enlarged in the 19th century, given two storeys of twin windows and decorated with coats-of-arms. The courtyard is interesting for its portico with massive pillars, its paintings, its statues and terracottas.

Opposite, the Palazzo del Comune is a solid stone construction which was built by the Guelfs in 1294 when Giano della Bella was Podestà and finished by the Ghibellines in 1334. The ground floor has a portico with tierspoint arcades with triple bays above twin windows and on the last storey.

In the interior there are several interesting rooms and a museum which is rich in Florentine Primitives and works by painters of Pistoia.

Taking Via Pacini, we reach the most remarkable building in Pistoia, the Ceppo Hospital which was founded in the 13th or 14th century. Then in the 16th century a Florentine-type portico was added, and Giovanni della Robbia decorated it with wonderful glazed terracottas. The tympanum of the entrance portal, on the door to the left of the portico, is the most ancient work (1510) and is by Buglioni who was a member of the della Robbia workshop. In the spandrels of the semicircular arcades, the medallions by Giovanni della Robbia and Santi Buglioni represent, notably, scenes from *The Life of the Virgin*. Above, a long frieze is devoted to *The Seven Acts of Mercy* which alternate with *The Cardinal and Theological Virtues*. The first six high-reliefs are by Santi Buglioni.

Taking Via del Ceppo, we reach the small Church of S. Maria delle Grazie built in 1452 from the design by Michelozzo, with its handsome portal and elegant cupola. We then continue to the Church of S. Bartolomeo in Pantano of 1159 with its beautiful unfinished Pisan façade which is decorated below with five blind arcades. The high-relief of 1167 on the lintel of the central portal is probably by Gruamonte. It represents *Christ Commanding the Apostles* and the figures seem to be derived from sculptures of Roman sarcophagi. The campanile with its ogival openings is resting on a truncated tower.

The interior has three high, narrow naves separated by columns and pillars with fine historiated capitals, and terminates in an apse which also is high and narrow. The central nave has a timbered roof. In the right nave we can admire the pulpit by Guido of Como (1250) which represents the transition of Romanesque art in Pistoia. The pulpit was badly reassembled when it was transported in 1591 from the central nave to its present site. Rectangular in shape, it is resting on three columns, two on lions and the central one on a crouching male figure. The bas-reliefs refer to *The Life of Christ* and the style rather recalls Classic antiquity.

We can see also the Church of S. Pietro Maggiore. The lower part of the façade and the left side are in the Pisan style and date from the 13th century. The lintel of the central portal with its statuettes in niches having columns is related to the Roman sarcophagi of the Late Empire.

Taking Via Palestro and Via Cavour where we see the Palazzo Panciatichi of 1313, we reach the Church of S. Giovanni Fuorcivitas, so named since it once stood beyond the city walls. It dates from the early 8th century, but work on the present building was not begun until the middle of the 11th century, continued during the following century and was finished in the 14th by Masters from Como.

The lateral façade with its bands of white and green marble is flanked by high arcades and above by two series of blind arcades. On the lintel of the portal there is a bas-relief which probably dates from 1162 and is signed by Gruamonte. It represents *The Last Supper*. Above, two lions are striking down a man and a bear. On the tympanum there is a statuette of *Saint John the Baptist* of 1345 by the Pisan School. The principal façade is unfinished.

The interior has a single nave and a timbered roof with a raised choir and a flat chevet with a triplet. We can admire a handsome large wooden *Christ on the Cross* of the 13th and 14th centuries, an equally handsome holy-water basin decorated with *The Cardinal and Theological Virtues* by Giovanni Pisano and a fine pulpit by Fra Guglielmo da Pisa, Nicola Pisano's pupil, finished in 1270. Rectangular in shape, it is resting on two consoles and two columns supported by lions. The bas-reliefs related to *The Life of Christ* have been inspired by Classic art and each scene has much atmosphere and dignity.

Of interest also, in the choir, are a large polyptych by Taddeo Gaddi and a wonderful *Visitation*, a terracotta which is attributed to Andrea della Robbia and Paolino del Signoraccio.

Since the very fine Church of S. Giovanni Battista by Ventura Vitoni was destroyed during the last war by American bombers, we will take Corso Umberto I in order to see the Church of S. Domenico which was built at the close of the 13th century.

The interior has a huge nave with a timbered roof, a transept with ogival vaulting and a flat chevet. Along the walls are tombs and the remains of frescoes. The altars have interesting paintings.

A door on the right leads to the large cloister, the chapter-house which is decorated with frescoes and the Cloister of la Maddalena, so called because the walls are decorated with frescoes by Vini, Rosselli and two others, referring to the life of the Saint. All that remains is a single gallery with 14th-century octagonal columns.

Let us continue our visit of the churches of Pistoia with that of S. Paolo in Corso Umberto I. This is a building in the Pisan style of 1291 with a lovely façade having a loggia and blind arcades. The rich portal is decorated on the tympanum with a sculpture by Jacopo di Mazzeo representing *Saint Paul Between Two Angels*. The interior, with its single nave and timbered roof, terminates in a polygonal apse.

We now head for the Madonna dell'Umiltà, a truly original building in the style of Brunelleschi by an architect of Pistoia named Ventura Vitoni. The interior is pleasantly designed with its richly decorated vestibule and octagon.

Taking Corso Vittorio Emanuele, we reach the large Church of S Francesco which was begun in 1294. Built in the form of a Latin cross, it has a huge nave with timbered roof and a large transept leading to five large chapels with ogival vaulting. On the walls are the remains of frescoes by the School of Giotto, notably in the choir, which was decorated by Puccio Campanna, Giotto's pupil, Lippo Memmi and Pietro Lorenzetti. The frescoes in the first chapel on the left are equally remarkable.

We can also see the cloister and the elegant chapter-house whose vaulting is decorated with frescoes by Puccio Capanna. Those on the wall are by other artists, including scenes of the foundation of S. Maria della Neve. Treated in curiously realistic manner, they are by Antonio Vite, an original master of the late 14th century.

On the other side of the *piazza*, Via S. Andrea leads us to the Church of S. Andrea, one of the most interesting in Pistoia. It has a beautiful 12th-century façade in the Pisan style whose upper part is unfinished, having five arcades and faced with white and green marble and inlaid work above the arcades. The lateral portals are decorated with animals and the principal portal with lions devouring a man and a monster, while on the tympanum there is a statue of Saint Andrew in the style of Giovanni Pisano. On the lintel, a bas-relief by Gruamonte and Adeodato (1166) represents *The Magi*. The historiated capitals are by a Master Enrico.

The interior has three very narrow naves, the central one being higher, and a timbered ceiling. The apse is oven-shaped. In the left nave, we can see a splendid pulpit by Giovanni Pisano which is considered his masterpiece. Hexagonal in form, it is similar to the one by his father, Nicola Pisano, in the Baptistery of Pisa, but the trilobulate arcades are tierspoint. Of the seven columns, two are resting on lions, one on a man bent over and the central one on a base which is framed by two eagles and a lion. The pulpit is decorated with statues of sibyls, prophets, angels and scenes from *The Life of Christ*. In this pulpit, which is a model of its kind, the sculptor has harmonised a tempestuous and pathetic quality with classical seriousness.

Finally, in the third chapel on the left, there is a fine wooden *Christ on the Cross* by Giovanni Pisano.

We can now take the *autostrada* for Florence but we must not miss a visit to PRATO, another Florentine town of outstanding artistic interest, notably for its Cathedral with the pulpit by Donatello and frescoes by Filippo Lippi.

This is a small industrial town, where the Bisenzio Valley opens on to the plain of Pistoia, surrounded by orchards, mulberry trees and olive groves.

The Cathedral is an elegant edifice. Work was begun in 1211 by Guidetto da Como who decorated the façade and the right side with arcades in the Pisan-Luccan style, and finished in the first half of the 14th century by an impressive transept with, opening on to it, five ogival chapels whose design is attributed to Giovanni Pisano.

The façade is faced with alternating horizontal bands of white and dark green marble of Prato. On the tympanum of the portal is a white terracotta *Madonna Between Saint Stephen and Saint Lawrence* by Andrea della Robbia.

On the right is the famous *Pulpit of the Holy Girdle* by Donatello and Michelozzo, a wonderful work of grace and vitality with its ring of little dancing *putti* in which movement is expressed with much verve and joy.

The right side is decorated above with blind arcades and flanked by Lombard bands between which there are two marble portals framed by columns. The campanile is a massive tower of 1340 whose three storeys of twin bays have been raised on two others having two or three bays, the work of Niccolo di Cecco del Mercia and his son, da Sano. The transept has a Gothic door.

The interior, which is severe and typically Romanesque, has three naves which are separated by massive columns of dark green marble. The vaulting dates from the 17th century. The pulpit of 1473 is an exuberant work by Mino da Fiesole assisted by Antonio Rossellino. It was Mino da Fiesole, however, who thought of a pulpit in the form of a chalice and who executed the two bas-reliefs representing *Herod's Feast* and *The Beheading of Saint John the Baptist* as well as the four supporting figures, the other bas-reliefs having been sculptured by Rossellino. The base with its sphinxes is probably by Pasquino di Matteo. The two bronze candelabra facing the choir are by Masso di Bartolomeo.

At the end of the three naves, there are six steps which lead to the transept with its high tierspoint arcades and ogival vaulting, which were decorated with frescoes by Domenico da Bologna in 1366.

On the high altar there is a large *Crucifix* by Tacca. The chancel is decorated with *Scenes from The Life of Saint John the Baptist* by Filippo Lippi, with its celebrated *Feast of Herod*, which best exemplifies the artist's element of homely poetry and inventive grace, for here he has portrayed a feast given by a wealthy Florentine noble of the 15th century. On the left wall is the *Life of Saint Stephen*. Filippo Lippi has included his own portrait and that of his assistant Fra Diamanto in the scenes of *The Burial of Saint Stephen*.

These frescoes, which exemplified the sort of narrative painting that was to mark this epoch, offer an occasion to mention their history and Fra Filippo Lippi, whose life was so characteristic of the Italian artists of that period. The first Italian painter to care greatly for the look of everyday people, he was born in Florence in 1406, orphaned at an early age, turned over to the Carmelite Order at the age of six and finally became a monk in 1421. As a young man he saw Masaccio painting his epoch-making frescoes in the Brancacci Chapel and this made him discover his true vocation as a painter. Recognising Fra Filippo Lippi's exceptional talent, his superiors authorised him to leave the convent in order to practise his art, yet still dressed as a monk. He attracted the attention of Cosimo de Medici who became his protector, for his life was hardly a model of chastity and discipline. (He later ran away with the nun, Lucrezia Buti, shuffled off his monastic vows and, through the indulgence of the humanist Pope Pius II, married and settled down as the father of a family.) Cosimo de Medici ordered several paintings from Fra Filippo Lippi and made him chaplain of Santa Margharita at Prato. It was in this convent that he discovered Lucrezia Buti who became the model for his *Virgins*. Later she gave birth to a son who became equally famous as Filippino Lippi.

In 1465 Fra Filippo Lippi was called to Spoleto and there, having begun a lovely apse decoration for the Cathedral, he died three years later, in 1469, and was buried. Lorenzo de Medici commissioned Filippino Lippi to design a handsome monument to his celebrated father.

The Cathedral of Prato has other interesting frescoes, notably in the first chapel to the right of the choir one which is the work of two 15th-century painters. Andrea di Giusto did *The Marriage of the Virgin* and *The Martyrdom and Burial of Saint Lawrence*. The other painter known as the Master of Prato (certain scholars have endeavoured to identify him as Paolo Uccello or one of his pupils) executed *The Birth of the Virgin*, *The Presentation in the Temple*, *Christ Disputing with the Elders* and *The Burial of Saint Lawrence*.

In the left arm of the Gothic transept is *The Death of Saint Jerome* by Fra Filippo Lippi (1452) and a tabernacle with *The Madonna of the Olive Tree* by Benedetto da Majano. In the first chapel of the left of the choir we can admire the frescoes by Agnolo Gaddi and in the second by an unknown 14th-century Master, also the fine tomb of Filippo Inghirami which is attributed to Simone di Niccolo de Beardi, said to be Donatello's brother.

Let us now visit the Chapel of the Holy Girdle which was built in 1385. The delightful wrought-iron grille was begun by Masso di Bartolomeo, continued by Antonio di Ser Cola and finished by Pasquino di Matteo of Montepulciano. The frescoes on the walls by Agnolo Gaddi and his pupils portray the legend of the holy girdle which was presented by the Virgin during the Assumption to Saint Thomas. On the altar there is a fine *Virgin and Child* by Giovanni Pisano.

From the left of the façade we reach the courtyard which has preserved a gallery of the cloister in the Florentine Romanesque style. It is built of marble, the white from Carrara and the green from Prato. The Opera del Duomo (or Cathedral Museum) is installed in a building on the left and contains several fine paintings and sculptures by Masso di Bartolomeo, Niccolo di Tommaso, and the remains of the original pulpit by Niccolo di Cecco del Mercia.

Taking Via Mazzoni we reach Piazza del Comune where we see the Palazzo Pretorio, a massive building with a flight of steps which seems to date from the 13th and 14th centuries. The most ancient part is that on the right, built of brick; it has preserved its tower-house aspect, while the part on the left, built of stone, has eight twin windows. The crenels and the small campanile were added in the 16th century.

In the interior, we can visit a museum that is rich in works by Filippo and Filippino Lippi, Bernardo Daddi, Botticini, Giovanni da Milano, Fra Bartolomeo and others.

Opposite, the Palazzo del Comune has unfortunately been remodelled, but the Council Room has preserved its ancient decoration with 15th-century frescoes and a 17th-century ceiling.

If we take Via Ricasoli with its 18th-century Library Palace, we will discover in a near-by street the Palazzo Datini which once belonged to F. Datini (1330–1410), one of the most important merchants and bankers of his period. The palace is a typical example of civic architecture of 15th-century Tuscany. The interior has preserved its fine mural decorations by Niccolo di Pietro Gerini, also the ancient archives of the Datini business house.

We then reach the Church of S. Francesco with its white and green bands and a 14th-century portal. The interior has a single nave and a timbered roof. At the far end, three ogival chapels have been restored to their original design, while in the choir we find the tombstone of F. Datini by Lamberti (1412).

We gain access, on the right, to the 15th-century cloister and the chapter-house which is completely decorated with frescoes by Niccolo di Pietro Gerini (1395).

In the square behind the church is the Basilica of S. Maria

PRATO, PULPIT OF THE HOLY
GIRDLE.

10. POPPI, PALAZZO PRETOR.

delle Carceri which was built following a miracle performed
by an image of the Virgin painted on the wall of the prison
which once stood on this site. This pleasant building in the
form of a Greek cross is by Giuliano da Sangallo and is faced
on the exterior with polychrome marble.

The interior has great majesty and harmonious proportions, with its impressive cupola richly decorated with glazed
terracottas by Andrea della Robbia, its serious *Evangelists* in
the pendentives and its frieze, all treated with grace and
elegance. Here Andrea della Robbia achieved a perfection
which he rarely equalled elsewhere.

Opposite stands the Castle of the Emperor, a fortress
which, except in Apulia, has no equal in Italy. Like the
Castel del Monte, it was built by Frederick II in 1237.
Square in plan, it is flanked by square towers at the angles
and others as buttresses. The walls are topped by Ghibelline
crenels and a fine portal leads to the interior.

Returning to Piazza S. Francesco, we will continue to the
Convitto Nationale Cicognini, whose college was founded in
1699 and included among its pupils the celebrated Italian
author Gabriel d'Annunzio. Next we find the Church of
S. Niccolo of 1322 with its handsome portal, then the
Church of S. Domenico of 1283 with its fine marble portal
and its 15th-century cloister. The galleries have several
tombs. It was in this convent that Savonarola spent two
years and Fra Bartolomeo became a monk.

Instead of travelling directly to Florence, we will cross the
plain and return to the N.66 at POGGIO A CAIANO in
order to see the luxurious Medici Villa surrounded by its
wonderful gardens, built by Lorenzo the Magnificent in 1480
from the design by Guiliano da Sangallo. Under Leo X and
the first great dukes of the House of Medici, it was restored
and enlarged.

The architecture is simple. The villa is merely a
rectangular building with a central part flanked by two

projecting wings; the ground floor is surmounted by two storeys and surrounded by a portico which runs along the entire ground floor, forming a terrace on the first storey, which was subsequently added.

In the centre of the façade, an Ionic portico with a triangular pediment decorated with glazed terracottas, opens on to a loggia with barrel-vaulting and decorated with masks and emblems, including the fragments of a *Sacrifice* by Filippo Lippi.

In the interior, we must admire, above all, the great central *salon*. The barrel-vaulted coffer ceiling is decorated with frescoes dealing with ancient history, but likewise referring to the generosity of Lorenzo the Magnificent, the celebrated patron of the arts.

In October 1587 the Grand Duke Francesco II, who had just recently started his liaison with Bianca Cappello, died in this villa in mysterious circumstances, doubtless poisoned together with his young consort, who expired several hours later.

Six kilometres away we can see another Medici villa at ARTIMINO which has preserved a crenellated tower and the remains of a mediaeval castle, the Villa di Artimino, which was built by Bernardo Buontalenti in 1594 for Ferdinand I. This is an impressive rectangular building whose severe façade, enlivened merely by a loggia, is flanked by two towers. A bathroom has retained some elegant frescoes by Bernardini Poccetti.

Near by we can see also the 10th- and 11th-century Church of S. Leonardo which, although mutilated in the 18th century, has preserved its campanile, its three apses and its lateral façades decorated with arcades. Two kilometres away, isolated in the open landscape, is the Church of S. Martino in Campo which once belonged to a Benedictine abbey and dates from the 9th and 10th centuries. The apsidal part was rebuilt after a fire which occurred in the 11th century. There are remains of frescoes.

SIGNA is a place known for its hat industry and its ceramics. The upper part has preserved the remains of its ramparts. On Piazza Cavour, the Church of S. Giovanni Battista has three naves, baptismal fonts of 1480 and the sarcophagus of the Blessed Giovanna di Signa. In Via Mazzini, the Oratory of S. Lorenzo has a splendid 11th-century pulpit and beautiful 14th-century frescoes.

We return to the N.66 at S. Pietro a Ponti and soon reach Florence.

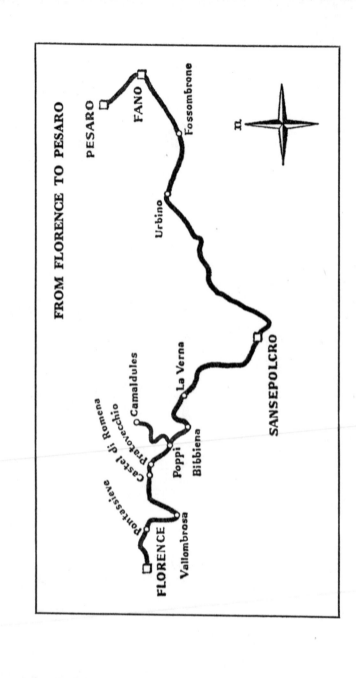

ITINERARY IV

FROM FLORENCE TO PESARO

Pontassieve — Vallombrosa — Castello di Romena —
S. Pietro di Romena — Poppi — Camaldoli — Bibbiena
— La Verna — Sansepolcro — Urbino — Fossombrone
— Fano.

WE leave Florence by the N.67 which follows the left bank of the Arno, passes through Rovezzano and leaves, on the left, at No. 511, the Villa Favard, now occupied by the Work of Divine Providence; the building was rebuilt by Baccio d'Agnolo in the 16th century. Then after Sieci we pass through REMOLE whose 11th-century Church of S. Giovanni Battista, flanked by an elegant campanile, has three naves. The 15th-century baptistery has preserved more ancient parts and the fine *Crucifixion* is by the workshop of Botticelli.

We reach PONTASSIEVE which suffered greatly during the last war; the parish church was destroyed and the Palazzo da Filicaia badly damaged. Of the ancient town walls there remains merely the Porta Fiorentina.

We will take the N.70 which ascends amidst vineyards and olive groves and find, immediately on the right, the road leading to the ABBEY OF VALLOMBROSA. The road passes through Pelago and enters an Alpine landscape, ascending across the State forest of Vallombrosa which, soon after the year 1000, was given to two monks of the Abbey of Settimo so that they might lead a hermit's life. In 1013 they were joined by a Florentine noble. The number increased and in 1040 they adopted a rule that was similar to the Benedictine one. In 1055 this new Order was recognised by Pope Victor II. The Order soon developed and was presented with important donations. The Abbots of Vallombrosa enjoyed the title of Count and in the 15th century that of Marchese di Monte Verde e di Canneto. In 1224 the oratory was rebuilt of stone and in the 15th century the Monastery was enriched with numerous works of art, but in 1529 the building was sacked by the troops of Charles V.

The Monastery we see before us dates therefore from the 15th century but it was enlarged in the following century and transformed in the 18th. This simple and restrained building is dominated by a high 13th-century campanile and a 15th-century tower which creates the aspect of a castle. It is fronted by a courtyard enclosed by walls and the gate has a fine wrought-iron grille of 1773. A second gate leads to a vestibule and to a small courtyard, at the far end of which stands the façade of the church, fronted by a portico.

The interior, which was remodelled in the 18th century, is in the form of a Latin cross and has a single nave with a cupola resting on eight Ionic columns, and two large lateral altars.

Of interest also are the principal cloister, the kitchen and the refectory.

At Consuma we will rejoin the N.70 which, as it descends, offers some fine views of the Casentino. At the end of ten kilometres, we take a small road on the left which heads for Pratovecchio and enables us to see the CASTELLO DI ROMENA, which was built in the 11th century and belonged to a branch of the House of Guidi. In 1280 during the time of the brothers Alessandro, Guido Pace and Aghinolfo, Master Adam da Brescia made counterfeit florins of the Republic of Florence. The Guidi di Romena, who had given Dante hospitality, sold the castle to the Republic of Florence in

1357. It was captured in 1440 by Niccolo Piccinino, then recaptured by Neri Capponi for the Counts of the House of Medici. A fine avenue of cypress trees leads to the castle. Of the original 14 towers, only three remain: the keep, the Postierla and the prison tower. Before us are the remains to the three *enceintes*. There is a fine view over the valley.

We will continue to Fonte Branda, the fountain mentioned by Dante in reference to Master Adam, near the Podesteria, a house which partly dates from the 13th century. Then reaching the bridge over the Arno, we reascend along a narrow road which crosses a forest of chestnut trees. S. PIETRO DI ROMENA is an interesting 12th-century church, replacing a more ancient one; it was damaged by an earthquake in 1729 and restored. The simple façade is flanked by a massive campanile. The apse has two series of semicircular blind arcades, two twin windows and another window with three bays.

The interior which is in the basilican plan has three naves with massive monolithic columns which swell out at the base and are surmounted by wonderful historiated or foliated capitals. The vaulting is timbered, the choir raised and the apse is oven-shaped.

On the walls we can see the remains of a triptych by Giovanni del Biondo and his school (1386), several Florentine works of the 15th century and in the sacristy a fine 13th-century *Madonna and Child with Two Angels* by the Master of Varlungo.

We descend towards the Arno, cross the river and reach Pratovecchio which was almost entirely destroyed during the last war.

We next take the road to Poppi, but one kilometre away at S. MARIA A POPPIENA, we can see also the ancient Benedictine abbey which was given in 1009 by Counts Alberto and Ugo di Romena to the prior of the Camaldulians, a religious order founded about 1012 by Saint Thomas at Camaldoli, near Arezzo. We can see the remains of the 12th-century construction on the exterior of the apse. The interior has a single nave with a timbered roof and an original stone apse. The fresco dates from the 12th century and the *Assumption* is by Giovanni da Ponte.

We next reach POPPI, a picturesque town with its streets bordered by porticos, and in the centre the small Church of la Madonna del Morbo of 1631. It is polygonal and enclosed on three sides by porticos. Alongside is the 17th-century Church of S. Marco.

We then find the wide esplanade known as the Pratello with the Palazzo Pretorio, the ancient castle of Counts Guidi, which was begun by Count Simone di Battifolle about 1274 and continued by Count Guido. In the centre of the façade, which is crowned with Guelf crenels, there rises a high tower. The more ancient part on the right has a storey with twin windows, while the one on the left has two storeys also with twin windows.

We cross the wide moat of the *enceinte*, pass beneath a portal of 1447 surmounted by a stone lion and enter a curious courtyard decorated with coats of arms, some in terracotta after the manner of della Robbia, of Florentine Commissars. To the left, the Florentine Marzocco in stone rests at the foot of a covered stairway.

On the first storey, the great reception room, with its wooden ceiling decorated with interesting paintings, is followed by the library rich in rare books, the chapel whose frescoes are attributed to Taddeo Gaddi or his school, and various other rooms.

At the far end of the palace we can see also the Devil's Tower, the early dwelling of the Guidi before the castle was built. Then taking Via Cavour we find the late 13th-century Church of S. Fedele. The façade has a portal surmounted by an oculus. The single nave interior is in the form of a Latin cross and has a timbered roof. There are several paintings, including a *Crucifixion* by the School of Giotto and a *Virgin and Child* by the Master of la Maddalena. The crypt has three naves resting on pillars.

From Poppi, we can visit the Monastery of the Camaldulians and the Hermitage. We have the choice of the poor road to Moggiani which is 15 kilometres long, or the one to Montanino which is but 13 and no better, or finally by way of Soci, taking the road to Bibbiena, the N.71, which we leave at the end of 14 kilometres in order to follow the one to Camaldoli which is but five kilometres away.

CAMALDOLI with its picturesque forest setting is a summer resort. Next is the Monastery of the Camaldulians and, three kilometres away, the Hermitage.

The entire territory was given by Count Maldolo of Arezzo (from which we have the name Cà Maldoli) to Saint Romualdo who, in 1012, built the first part of the Hermitage and several years later the Foresteria. After the death of Saint Romualdo in 1027, the community he had founded soon increased and in 1080 the fourth prior of the Camaldulians, the Blessed Rodolfo, codified the Rule which is followed to this day.

Consisting of 1,442 hectares, the forest is impressive and solemn, especially that part lying between the monastery and the hermitage.

The Monastery, which is picturesquely situated, was built after 1012 on the site of the ancient castle of Count Maldolo of Arezzo. After being used as a guest-house and a hospice, it was enlarged, then made into a monastery which could house about 100 monks. After being destroyed twice by fire, it was rebuilt in 1203 and again in 1276. This is a massive, irregular building which consists of the monastery, the church and the guest-house and is fronted by a large square. Opposite, there extends the façade of the ancient guest-house which has a fine square courtyard bordered by porticos whose columns date from the 10th and 11th centuries, also a

15th-century cloister which is enclosed on two sides by galleries having elegant columns.

Entrance to the monastery is on the left. We find ourselves in a courtyard with, on the right, a mediaeval building with 13th-century and 14th-century windows and, at the far end, the church which was built in the first half of the 11th century, then rebuilt in the 16th and enlarged in the 18th.

The Baroque interior has a single nave and is decorated with frescoes and paintings by Vasari and Pacini.

Only male visitors are permitted in the refectory of 1572 with its carved wooden ceiling by Giovanni Dominici and its 15th-century frescoes, the cloister of 1543 and the pharmacy.

We then reach the EREMO DI CAMALDOLI, which is the original hermitage of Saint Romualdo. The portal with the Chapel of S. Antonio on the left leads to a small courtyard which is flanked by low buildings with, at the far end, the church which was consecrated in 1027 but rebuilt in 1658 and 1708. The Baroque façade is flanked by two towers. The single-nave church is divided by a richly-carved wooden screen and the walls are decorated with frescoes.

Of interest also is the refectory of 1679 and 20 monks' cells which are arranged in five rows, each having its own small portico. Each has its history and can be visited in detail.

We return to the N.71 and continue to ascend the valley of the Arno which flows between wooded hills.

BIBBIENA has several interesting palaces, notably the large Palazzo Dovizi at No. 26, Via Dovizi. This early 16th-century building is a fine example of rustic Tuscan architecture with its elegant portal and its two rows of windows, those above being flanked by columns. The Church of S. Lorenzo is of 1474 and that of SS. Ippolito et Donato dates from the 12th century but was remodelled at different periods. In the transept we can see one of the rare paintings by Arcangelo di Cola da Camerino, *The Virgin and Child and Angels*.

We now take a small road, the N.208, which by way of
Dama crosses a wood of chestnut trees to LA VERNA where
the monastery has a guest house; but we can also spend the
night close by at La Beccia.

La Verna is a strange chalk peak which is very steep on
one side and which is covered with a forest of age-old pine
trees. It is famous for its natural beauties and its memories
of Saint Francis.

In 1213 Count Orlando dei Cattani, who then owned the
wild and deserted mountain, offered it to Saint Francis of
Assisi who spent two years here with a handful of his companions and built cabins of wood and clay. It was here on
24th September 1224 that Saint Francis received the
stigmata. La Verna soon became one of the principal centres
of the Franciscan Order. A great convent was built and
attracted crowds of pilgrims.

After passing various rather uninteresting buildings, we
enter a courtyard and discover at the far end the Church of
S. Maria degli Angeli which was built in 1216 by Count
Orlando but subsequently modified. The simple façade is
flanked by a small modern campanile and the single-nave
interior with ogival vaulting is decorated with glazed terracottas which are attributed to Giovanni della Robbia. The
second part of the church, the more ancient one, is enclosed
by simple Renaissance stalls and the forealtar is a wonderful
work by Andrea della Robbia.

We next reach the Chiesa Maggiore. Begun in 1348, this
simple church was damaged during the last war. The portico
which had been added in the 16th century has been almost
entirely rebuilt.

The Renaissance interior has a nave with ogival vaulting
and deep side-chapels. There are several works of art,
including two superb glazed terracottas by Andrea della
Robbia representing *The Annunciation* and *The Adoration of the
Shepherds*, and numerous reliquaries.

Leaving the church we enter the Chapel of the Count of Motedoglio and reach the Corridor of the Stigmata whose walls are decorated with frescoes portraying the life of Saint Francis. We then descend to a somewhat theatrical grotto which was the cell of Saint Francis with its stone bed. There are different chapels, including the Chapel of the Stigmata of 1263, and several others scattered in the forest.

We can visit also the convent whose buildings are arranged around five cloisters.

We now take the road to Pieve S. Stefano at the junction of the Ancione and the Tevere. The town was almost entirely destroyed by the Germans when they retreated in 1944. The Palazzo Comunale has been rebuilt in its original form with, on the left, a curious tower with machicolation.

SANSEPOLCRO has preserved several fine palaces, like the Palazzo Pichi-Sermolli with its mediaeval tower and the Palazzo delle Laud, on the left of the Cathedral, which was begun by Alberti in 1591 and finished by Catagallina in 1609.

The Cathedral, which was built in 1012 but remodelled at subsequent periods, has the restrained stone façade of the original building with its three portals and its large rose-window. The interior has three naves, the central one with timbered vaulting. There are interesting 14th- and 15th-century works of art.

Sansepolcro is the birthplace of Piero della Francesca. In the Picture Gallery we can admire his wonderful *Resurrection* and splendid polyptych, *The Virgin of Mercy with Several Saints*, *The Annunciation* and *The Crucifixion* as well as the predella with its *Scenes from the Passion*. In addition, there are several works attributed to Piero della Francesca and his workshop.

We can see also the Church of S. Francesco of 1258 with, on the façade, a trilobulate Gothic portal and a large rose-window. The interior has a single nave. We then reach the cloister and the ancient 13th-century chapter-house with its Gothic portal flanked by two twin windows.

Opposite, the Church of la Madonna delle Grazie is of 1518, while that of S. Agostino, which was rebuilt in 1771, has preserved its 16th-century portal and a Romanesque campanile.

We continue to follow the N.3 *bis* for four kilometres and at S. GIUSTINO we can see the Bufalini Castle which was made into a villa by Vasari. It is fairly well preserved, including the inner decoration by Gherardi.

We next take the N.73 *bis* on the left for Urbino which makes winding ascents with fine views over the fertile Tiber Basin which is entirely planted with trees. Our winding road passes through Bocca Trabaria and we reach Lamoli whose church, which is that of the Benedictine Abbey of S. Michele delle Lamule, has preserved a Romanesque apse.

The road becomes straight again and we arrive at MERCATELLO which has partly preserved its mediaeval aspect. The Romanesque-Gothic Church of S. Francesco is a simple building with, on the tympanum of the portal, a 15th-century fresco by the Umbrian School, *The Betrothal of Saint Catherine and Saint Francis*. The interior, which has a single nave with a timbered roof and a quadrangular apse, contains the handsome tomb of Bartolomeo Brancaleoni of 1424 with a Gothic baldachin having two polylobulate arcades, and various paintings by Giovanni Baronzio.

On the right we can see the ancient chapter-house and farther on, the Palazzo Gasparini of 1640 and the Collegiate Church which has three naves and was completely rebuilt.

S. Angelo in Vado is a small town which has preserved its ancient aspect together with various palaces and churches which, although interesting, I shall not attempt to describe. Next is Urbania which also has several churches of secondary interest. In the Church of S. Francesco which was built in the 13th century but remodelled in the 18th, we can see a fine

Crucifixion by Pietro di Rimini. The Ducal Palace, which was built in the 13th century but transformed in the 15th, has a beautiful Renaissance courtyard.

After numerous curves in the road, we reach URBINO which is the highlight of this itinerary. It is the birthplace of Raphael and Bramante, and its Ducal Palace is one of the masterpieces of the Renaissance.

We enter the town beneath the Porta di Valbona and see, rising before us on the right, above the large market place, the impressive Ducal Palace.

Taking Via Mazzini, we reach Piazza VIII Settembre and after making a right turn we discover the *ensemble* of buildings which comprise the Archbishop's Palace, the Cathedral and the Ducal Palace. The Palace glorifies the name of Federigo Montefeltro and his architect Luciano Laurana who made the ancient castle into an elegant and distinctive work. The building which faces the square has exquisite proportions with its decoration by Ambrosio Barocci. About 1474 work ended at the second courtyard and the last storey was built by Girolamo Genga about 1563. The Palace is now the seat of the National Gallery of the Marches.

The first courtyard, which is one of Luciano Laurana's most harmonious works, has two storeys of galleries, the second having been added after the death of Duke Federigo. An inscription in Latin which runs along the upper part of the portico with its elegant capitals, praises "the celebrated Federigo Montefeltro, Duke of Urbino and Count of Castel Durante, who built this palace, invincible warrior, a prince who was just, merciful and liberal".

An arcade leads to the monumental staircase which Vasari describes as the finest one of his time. Designed by Laurana and decorated by Barocci, it leads to the first storey where we can admire the doors and their sculptured frames, the windows and the panelling, notably in the Duke's study. They are attributed to Baccio Pontelli, Francesco di Giorgio

Martini and Botticelli. The walls are decorated with portraits of famous men by Justus van Ghent and Pedro Berruguete, many of which are now in the Louvre, and it would indeed be a fine thing if they were returned to their original place to complete the collection with those which have been returned from Rome.

Among the paintings which decorate the different rooms, the most important are those by Piero della Francesca, *The Holy Communion* by Justus van Ghent, *The Profanation of the Host* by Paolo Uccello, a *Portrait of a Gentleman* by Raphael and works by Titian and Signorelli.

Alongside, the Cathedral, begun in 1447 by Luciano Laurana, was badly damaged by an earthquake in 1789 and finally finished in 1801.

Opposite the Palace, the Church of S. Domenico has a grandiose portal by Masaccio (1449) with, on the tympanum, a wonderful terracotta by Luca della Robbia. The Gothic interior was dressed up in the Baroque taste by Vanvitelli in 1727. Facing the church is a small Egyptian obelisk which dates from the XXVI Dynasty (about 595 B.C.).

If we return to Piazza VIII Settembre, we will see the Church of S. Francesco. It dates from the second half of the 14th century but has preserved merely the portico of the façade, the interior having been rebuilt by Vanvitelli. In the apse, we can admire *The Pardon of Saint Francis* by Barocci.

We follow Via Raffaello with, at No. 57, the artist's house; a visit here is a touching experience, for we can see the bed in which he was born and the stone on which he ground his pigments.

Urbino is rich in palaces, notably in Via Barocci where the Oratory of S. Giuseppe has an attractive crib by Barocci. The Church of S. Giovanni Battista has a ceiling in the form of a ship's hull and the wonderful frescoes with their unsophisticated realism are by Jacopo and Lorenzo Salimbeni.

Taking the valley of the Metauro we will continue to

CALMAZZO and cross the Metauro over the Bridge of Trajan which has three arches, but has preserved merely an arcade and a pillar of the original construction. Five kilometres away we can find the Galleria del Furlo which in ancient times was known as *petra pertusa* or *forulus*, the origin of the name Furlo. It was dug in A.D. 76 at the narrowest place in the gorge to create the easiest opening for the Via Flaminia.

From Calmazzo we can continue to FOSSOMBRONE, a pleasant town spread out on the slopes of a hill. It has preserved several interesting monuments and palaces of the 15th and 16th centuries, notably the Renaissance Palazzo Albani which is partly attributed to Francesco Martini. It stands opposite the Cathedral which was rebuilt in the 18th century. Taking an arcade we reach the Corte Alta, built in 1464 by Federigo Montefeltro, which has been dismantled, with its quadrangular keep and its angle towers.

The valley gradually widens and we soon reach FANO, which I shall describe in one of my further volumes, and from there we take the coast road as far as Pesaro.

. MONASTERY OF LA VERNA.

. AREZZO, CHURCH OF S. MICHELE.

ITINERARY V

FROM FLORENCE TO ROME
BY WAY OF AREZZO AND PERUGIA

*Cascia — Gropina — Arezzo — Cortona — Farneta —
Castel Rigone — Magione — Perugia — Assisi —
Spello — Foligno — Sassovivo — Bevagna — Mantefalco
— Todi — Narni — Magliano Sabino — Civita
Castellana — Faleri — Nepi — Castel S. Elia — Veii.*

I AM now going to describe two itineraries from Florence
to Arezzo. The one which travels along the N.69 and
the Arno Valley is not very interesting, but the other which
follows the chain of the Pratomagno will enable us to see,
notably, the beautiful Romanesque Church of Gropina.

We can follow the N.69 as far as the outskirts of Montevarchi and there take the road which crosses the Arno and
heads directly for Lozo, Ciufferra and Gropina.

*

*   *

By our first route we leave Florence along the N.67 which
follows the Arno or along a shorter and less crowded road
which by way of Bagno a Ripoli, Meoste and Palazzio
returns to it at Incisa in Val d'Arno.

In Itinerary IV, I have described the road as far as
Pontassieve. We will continue to follow the Arno and at
S. Ellero leave, to the left, the road to the Abbey of Vallom-
brosa.

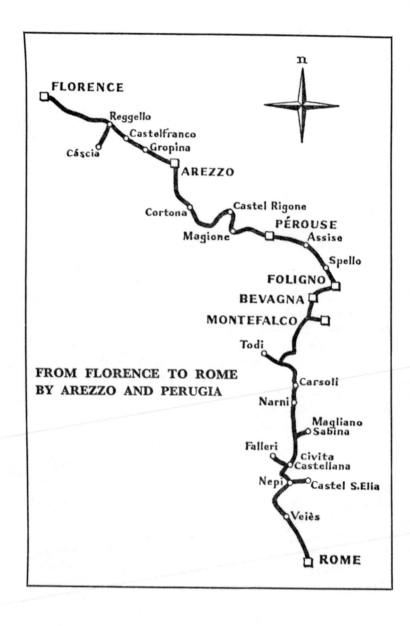

n

FLORENCE

Reggello

Castelfranco

Gropina

Cáscia

AREZZO

Cortona

Castel Rigone

PÉROUSE

Magione

Assise

Spello

FOLIGNO

BEVAGNA

MONTEFALCO

Todi

FROM FLORENCE TO ROME
BY AREZZO AND PERUGIA

Carsoli

Narni

Magliano
Sabina

Falleri

Civita
Castellana

Nepi

Castel S. Elia

Veiès

ROME

The village of S. Ellero has preserved a castle and an
ancient Cluniac abbey which has been transformed into a
factory.

This valley is quite charming with its many villages and
castles. Five kilometres after S. Ellero, we see, on the left,
the Villa Sammezzano which was given by Cosimo I to
Gian Giacomo de Medici de Marigano and acquired by
Fernando Ximenes of Aragon in 1605. In the 19th century it
was made into a Moorish villa.

We next see the massive Castellano Tower with its crenellated walls dating from the 12th and 13th centuries. We pass
through Incisa with its castle and its ancient bridge over the
Arno, rebuilt after the last war. In 1529 Lucrezia Mazzanti
jumped from this bridge to escape from the soldiers of the
Prince of Orange.

After crossing the Arno, the valley widens and we soon
reach FIGLINE VALDARNO whose early 12th-century
Collegiate Church was rebuilt in 1252 and transformed at the
close of the 15th century.

The interior has a single nave with a timbered roof.
We can admire a fine *Virgin and Child with Angels and Two
Saints* by the Master of Figline, a 14th-century painter also
known as the Master of the *Pietà*, now in the Fogg Art
Museum in the United States.

At No. 1, Via Castel Guinelli, we can see also a beautiful
15th-century house with a courtyard and the Church of
S. Francesco, dating from the middle of the 14th century and
remodelled in the 17th, with a simple façade fronted by a
portico. The pillars are octagonal. The single-nave interior
with large Gothic windows has frescoes by the School of
Botticelli. Of interest also are the cloister and the chapter-
house, whose fresco is perhaps by the same Master of
Figline.

We then pass through S. GIOVANNI VALDARNO
where we can see the Palazzo Pretorio enclosed by a portico

surmounted by a loggia and flanked by a crenellated tower. The 15th-century Basilica of S. Maria delle Grazie has a façade of 1840. A late 14th-century *Virgin* painted in fresco is the object of veneration.

Farther on, at MONTEVARCHI, the Collegiate Church, which was rebuilt in the 18th century, has alongside a small museum which contains interesting works of art.

*
* *

On our alternative route we will follow the N.67 as far as Rignano and two kilometres farther on take the road, on the left, for Leccio and Reggello. There is no need to go as far as Reggello. Shortly before, we make a right turning in order to see the church of CASCIA.

The façade is fronted by a wonderful portico with five semicircular arcades resting on massive columns with vigorously carved foliated capitals. The gable is decorated with delicate blind arcades. The interior has three naves which are separated by columns with fine composite capitals.

We return to the road from Reggello to Castelfranco di Sopra on the slopes of the Pratomagno which are covered with olive groves and offer fine views over the Arno Valley.

Before reaching Pian di Seo, we see on the left the ancient ABBEY OF SOFFENA which was built about the year 1000 and is now a farm. The church was rebuilt in 1394 and modified in the 16th century. It is flanked on the right by a campanile.

The interior which is in the form of a Greek cross has brick vaulting which creates a curious perspective effect. On the walls are remains of frescoes which date from the first half of the 15th century.

The cloister of the ancient Vallombrosan abbey has been preserved with its arcades resting on pillars.

We pass through Pian di Seo whose Romanesque church

has a façade decorated with blind arcades. In the interior, there are fine historiated capitals.

After vineyards and olive groves, we reach Castelfranco di Sopra which has preserved part of its ancient walls and two of its original four gates. In the centre, the church, which was built in the 13th century but remodelled in the 18th, is fronted by an elegant 15th-century portico.

We next pass through Certignano and, opposite the road to Montemarciano, we find the 16th-century Church of la Madonna delle Grazie which is enclosed by an elegant portico resting on columns.

The interior, with its single nave and timbered roof, has on the high altar a fine fresco which was painted by Masaccio when he was quite young (about 1420). The subject is *The Virgin Enthroned Feeding the Infant Child between Two Saints.*

We reach Loro Ciufenna, an ancient-looking town lying on a spur between two torrents. In the Church of S. Maria Assunta, we can see a triptych by Lorenzo di Bicci and other 16th-century works of art.

Somewhat farther on we find the interesting Romanesque parish church of GROPINA. The Church of S. Pietro, which was built (or rebuilt) in the 12th century, is remarkable for its apse which is decorated in the interior as well as on the exterior by blind arcades. On the exterior, they are surmounted by a gallery resting on columns. In the centre, there are two slender columns tied together. In the interior, the two storeys of galleries have taken their inspiration from Luccan art.

The interior, which is in the basilican form, has three naves which are separated by monolithic columns having curious capitals, many historiated. Those on the left are of a regional art which can be seen in other buildings of the same period, but those on the right show much originality. Their flat-tanned relief, their spiral ornamentation and their monsters indicate that they may be Pre-Romanesque. The pulpit is remarkable and entirely covered with bas-reliefs of mermaids and monsters.

We descend towards the fertile plain of Arezzo and passing the Porta S. Clemente, we reach the Porta S. Lorentino.

AREZZO is one of the most interesting towns in Tuscany and famous, above all, for the frescoes by Piero della Francesca in the Church of S. Francesco.

We must take Via Cavour which leads to the church which was begun in 1290 from the design by Fra Giovanni da Pistoia. It is built of brick with a plain façade having a portal and a rose-window.

A large Gothic nave with timbered roof is flanked, on the right, by Gothic and Renaissance aedicules and, on the left, by Gothic chapels. Beneath the paving are numerous tombstones and the walls are covered with frescoes. Those on the other side of the façade are by Giovanni d'Agolo di Balduccio, notably, *The Meal at the Home of Simon the Pharisee*, while the stained-glass window by Guglielmo de Marcillat represents *Honorius III Approving the Rule of Saint Francis* (1524).

On the right wall we see in turn a damaged fresco by Lorentino d'Arezzo, a *Crucifixion* by Giovanni d'Agnolo di Balduccio, a fresco in very bad condition by Soggi, Perugino's pupil, and after several others a fine *Annunciation* by Spinello Aretino.

In the choir we find the work on which Piero della Francesca's fame chiefly rests, the fresco cycle portraying *The Story of the True Cross* which he executed at the height of his powers between 1452 and 1466, inspired by Jacques de Voragine's *Golden Legend*. This is one of the outstanding masterpieces of Renaissance art, a work of great originality in which form and perspective are subordinated to the artist's desire for harmonious design. The deliberate stiffness of the figures exerts a strong and mysterious attraction. An author of mathematical treatises on perspective, Piero della Francesca turned to a monumental style in order to express his aesthetic conception of the world, one in which life flows to a rhythm so slow that it already seems to belong to eternity.

The scenes from the legend of the Holy Cross include *The Death of Adam*, *The Visit of the Queen of Sheba to King Solomon*, *The Transportation of the Wood of the Cross*, *Constantine's Dream*, *Constantine's Victory over Maxentius*, *The Invention and Proof of the True Cross*, *The Battle of the Emperor Heraclius Against Chosroes*, *The Cross Brought to Jerusalem* with, in addition, *The Annunciation* and two *Prophets*.

In the chapel on the left, is an *Annunciation*, an early work by Luca Signorelli who was influenced by Piero della Francesca, and on the left wall the monument of the jurisconsult Roselli by Michele da Firenze and a large *Crucifixion with Saint Francis at the Feet of Christ*.

We next take Corso Italia with its several palaces—at No. 209 is the Restaurant Cecco whose food is especially good—and finally the Pieve di Santa Maria which is the most outstanding religious building in Arezzo. An early one destroyed in 1111 was rebuilt later in the 12th century, remodelled in the Gothic style in the early 14th century and subsequently transformed.

The façade, which shows much originality, has five large blind arcades surmounted in the Pisan style by three storeys of loggias with horizontal crowning. The three portals have tympanums decorated with bas-reliefs, the central one framed by *The Labours of the Months*, the work of a 13th-century artist who was probably French.

On the angle of the façade, the campanile is a severe and massive tower with five storeys of semicircular twin windows.

The interior, with three naves which are separated by columns and a timbered roof, has tierspoint arcades, a high cupola and a raised choir above a crypt, which has five naves. This choir belongs to the early Romanesque building. We can admire a splendid polyptych by Pietro Lorenzetti which is signed and dated 1320. On the other side of the central portal, a fine bas-relief of the 12th or 13th century represents *The Epiphany*.

The apse, which faces Piazza Grande bordered by houses and mediaeval towers, is Romanesque, like the façade, and equally remarkable, with its high blind arcades which are surmounted by two rows of loggias.

On this same *piazza* we can see a public fountain, the Palazzo della Fraternità dei Laici of the 14th and 15th centuries. This palace was built by the Brotherhood of Charity during the time of Saint Francis. The façade, which was begun in the Gothic style and finished during the Renaissance, has great harmony with its splendid semi-circular portal surmounted by a bas-relief by Bernardo Rosellino representing *The Virgin of Mercy* between two niches with saints, its balustrade resting on consoles, and its loggia.

At the far end, the severe Palazzo delle Logge with its portico is by Vasari.

Taking Via dei Pileati, we reach the 14th-century Palazzo Pretorio which is decorated with emblems of podestàs, then the Palace of the Captains of the People of 1278. At No. 28 Via dell'Orto is the house in which Petrarch is said to have lived. It was destroyed when the Americans bombed Arezzo but has since been rebuilt.

We reach the ancient fortress which was built after the revolt of 1502 by Giuliano and Antonio da Sangallo for Cosimo de Medici but dismantled by the French. We next find the Cathedral which is a Romanesque-Gothic edifice that was remodelled at different periods. The façade is modern. On the exterior, only the 14th-century lateral portal is interesting. In the interior, we can see, in the choir, the reliquary of Saint Donat of 1369 with scenes from the life of the saint, then in the left nave the large tomb of Guido Tarlati di Pietramala, the warlike Bishop of Arezzo, built from the design by Giotto, and in the Chapel of the Madonna terracottas by Andrea della Robbia, Renaissance stained-glass windows and, above the door of the sacristy, a fresco by Piero della Francesca portraying *Mary Magdalene*.

On the other side of the square, the Palazzo dei Priori of 1333 is crowned by crenels and flanked by a massive quadrangular tower with machicolation.

Taking Via di Sasso Verde which is bordered by ancient houses, we can see the Church of S. Domenico which is a simple Gothic building. In the choir, we will find a grandiose *Crucifix* by Cimabue. It is the artist's oldest work and one of ardent and dramatic expression.

We reach Via XX Settembre with, at No. 55, the house of Vasari who decorated the walls with frescoes. We should not fail to see the Chamber of Fame and, above all, the Chamber of Apollo. The house has been made into a museum devoted to Vasari, including letters by famous Renaissance personages.

Next is the Church of S. Maria in Gradi which was built in the 12th century and rebuilt in 1592. There are terracotta by Andrea della Robbia. Taking Via Piaggia di Murello, we reach Via Lorentino with, at No. 8, the Renaissance Palazzo della Dogana which is attributed to Rossellino. It is now a Picture Gallery and has many interesting but second-rate works of art.

Near by in Via Garibaldi, we can see also the Renaissance Church of Santissima Annunziata and the Benedictine Badia di San Fiore with, on the high altar, a *Feast of Ahasuerus* by Vasari.

There now remains to be seen the Roman Amphitheatre and the Archaeological Museum, which is extremely interesting for its Etruscan collections.

South of Arezzo stands the Church of S. Maria delle Grazie which was begun in 1449. At the close of the century, Benedetto da Majano built the graceful portico which is in front. The single-nave interior has ogival vaulting, and the high altar of marble and glazed terracotta is by Andrea della Robbia.

We will take the N.71 for CASTIGLIONE FIOREN-TINO which is spread out on the slopes of a hill. On a *piazza* with its loggia of 1560, the early 16th-century Palazzo Comunale contains the Picture Gallery which has several interesting paintings and works of art.

We can see also the Romanesque-Gothic Church of S. Francesco which has a beautiful stone façade. The interior has a single nave and the cloister is enclosed by low arcades which are surmounted by elegant loggias. The Church of la Madonna della Consolazione is an octagonal Renaissance building. In a chapel of the ancient parish church there is a fine fresco by Luca Signorelli.

We then pass at the foot of CORTONA, a town which is rather disappointing, for the buildings are second rate. On the main square we find the Palazzo Comunale which was built in the 13th century, enlarged and badly restored. The Palazzo Pretorio contains a museum with Etruscan objects which were discovered during excavation. Opposite the mutilated Cathedral is a diocesan museum with several interesting works of art by Fra Angelico and Lorenzetti. The churches offer little interest with the exception perhaps of that of S. Nicole with its painting by Luca Signorelli. But all this is hardly worth the steep climb to a town which I found not very hospitable.

Ten kilometres from the road is the ABBEY OF FAR-NETA which was founded in the 9th century and formerly included a large number of buildings, a church, a cloister and a monastery. All that remains is a single church which was mutilated during the 18th century. The interior has a single nave with light ensured by Pre-Romanesque type bays, a timbered roof and a raised choir above the crypt. The interior terminates in three semicircular radiating apses and two others which have been added to the crossings.

But the chief interest of Farneta is the crypt which was disclosed during recent excavation and probably dates from the close of the 10th century. It has three naves which are separated by antique columns surmounted by original or resculptured capitals and two apses facing each other.

We reach the banks of Lake Trasimeno, leaving, on the left, the road to CASTIGLIONE DEL LAGO with its well-preserved fortified castle and its massive triangular keep. Entrance is from the ancient Ducal Palace by means of a curious covered passage which is wide enough only for one person at a time.

On the other side of the lake, the road passes through Passignano with a fine view of the lake, but the religious buildings are not very interesting.

Three kilometres farther on, we can take the road on the left which ascends to CASTEL RIGONE, a picturesque town which has preserved the remains of a castle rebuilt in 1297, and the Church of la Madonna dei Miracoli, a charming Renaissance building with its fine portal by Domenico Bertini da Settignano. The interior is richly decorated with frescoes and works of art with, in the apse, a curious cornice by Bernardino di Lazzaro of Perugia.

We descend to MAGIONE where we can see the *Badia* or Castle of the Knights of Malta. This is a 16th-century construction on a square plan with a courtyard having three storeys of loggias on three sides. The architect was the Bolognese Fieravante Fieravanti.

We soon reach PERUGIA, the capital of Umbria, the ancient Etruscan city and one of the most fascinating places in central Italy.

Perugia is built around a central *piazza* with its principal monuments which were the symbols of civic pride and power, while the slopes of the steep hill are covered with a network of winding streets and fortified houses. In the Middle Ages,

Perugia bristled with towers and its emblem was the griffin, which represented its fierce and warlike mood.

The people massacred the nobles. The nobles killed each other; the most powerful, the Baglioni, after destroying all their rivals, finally destroyed each other.

Piazza del Municipio, the pride of Perugia, is one of the most monumental *piazze* in all Italy with its Fountain, its Cathedral, its Archbishop's Palace and Palazzo Comunale, and its Palace of the College of Notaries.

The Fontana Maggiore, dating from 1277–1280, is one of the finest fountains of that period in Italy. Designed with elegance and harmony, it is one of those precious jewels which the Italians loved to embody in the heart of their cities, combining the splendour of water with that of stone. The fountain was executed by Nicola and Giovanni Pisano, probably with the aid of Arnolfo di Cambio. It consists of three superimposed basins, the last one of bronze resting on a slender column, which are topped by a delightful bronze group by Giovanni Pisano representing *Three Nymphs Carrying an Amphora*. The two other basins are of marble and polygonal in shape; the one is decorated with bas-reliefs representing *The Months of the Year, The Liberal Arts, Adam and Eve Driven from Paradise, Samson, The Fables of Aesop*, separated by slender columns. The other is decorated with statuettes which are all by Giovanni Pisano.

The Cathedral of San Lorenzo is a Gothic edifice which was begun in 1345 and finished in 1490. It is fronted by a bronze statue of Julius III by Vincenzo Danti (1555). The portal has been dressed up in the Baroque taste. A small 15th-century pulpit is composed of more ancient fragments.

The interior has three naves which are separated by octagonal pillars, tierspoint arcades and a polygonal apse.

On the reverse side of the façade, we can see the tomb of Bishop of Baglioni, who died in 1451, which is attributed to

Urbano da Cortona; in the choir are 15th-century stalls, and a 16th-century episcopal pulpit; and, in the left nave, a *Pietà* by Agostino di Duccio.

The Picture Gallery has merely one first-class work of art, *The Virgin Enthroned Between Several Saints* by Luca Signorelli.

At the side of the Cathedral, we find the Loggia di Bracio Fortebraccio of 1423, the 15th-century Seminary Palace, the Archbishop's Palace with its remains of the Podestà's Palace which was burnt in 1534. From the right side of the palace there is an interesting view, evocative of what Perugia was like in the Middle Ages with the small Church of la Maestà delle Volte, the arcade of an ancient palace with a Gothic portal, and a 13th-century tower-house.

The most outstanding building in the *piazza* is the Palazzo Comunale (or dei Priori). Begun in 1298, it was enlarged and completed two centuries later. The most ancient part facing the *piazza* is also the most picturesque, with its large portal which is flanked by triple bays and topped by statues of the Griffin and the Guelf Lion, its storey of triple Gothic bays, and its crowning of crenels and machicolation.

In Corso Vannucci the façade has a wonderful richly-decorated semicircular portal and beautiful Gothic windows with three bays, like those of the *piazza*.

In the interior, we see the great Hall of Notaries with eight semicircular bays decorated with frescoes by P. Cavallini or one of his pupils (1297). Another Hall has a fresco by Pinturicchio and a third a fresco by Dono Doni.

On the third floor is the Picture Gallery with its fine collection of works by Umbrian and Sienese painters. In the first room we find works by 13th-century artists, then the ancient Chapel of the Priors which was decorated in 1454 by Benedetto Bonfigli. The other rooms contain works by Gentile da Fabriano, Faddeo di Bartolo, Bartolo di Fredi, Fra Angelico, Piero della Francesca, Benozzo Gozzoli, Giovanni

Boccati, Bonfigli, Firenzo di Lorenzo, Agostino di Duccio, Perugino, Luca Signorelli and others.

In Corso Vannucci, the widest and most popular street in Perugia, we can see the remains of the Palace of the College of Notaries with its handsome Gothic portal, and the Collegio del Cambio, the old chamber of commerce, with the Udienza del Cambio, containing the celebrated frescoes by Perugino which he executed at the height of his career from 1498 to 1507. In payment he received 350 gold ducats. Raphael was probably one of the many pupils who helped him in the project. The theme, which was proposed by the humanist Francesco Maturanzo, tends to show that man's ability to achieve perfection is due to the fact that Christ made himself man and that harmony is attained by combining Classical culture and Christian sentiment.

This theme inspired Perugino to combine mythical divinities and Classical figures with religious iconography.

We then enter the chapel which was entirely painted by a pupil of Perugino named Giannicola di Paolo, who was influenced by Raphael.

We reach Piazza Matteoti which has several interesting buildings, including the 15th-century Palace of the Old University, the Palazzo del Capitano del Popolo, which dates from the Renaissance, with, at No. 6, an arcade leading to a terrace from which we can see other arcades which support the two palaces.

On this same *piazza* we find also the ancient Church of S. Maria del Popolo. Then taking Piazza Piccinino, we reach the Church of S. Severo which was built in 1007 on the site of a Temple of the Sun, but rebuilt in the 18th century. In the chapel Raphael painted his first independent fresco (1505). Although it betrays the influence of Fra Bartolomeo's *Last Judgment* in Florence, Raphael is already endeavouring to free himself of Perugino's effeminate style for a more vigorous one of his own.

The Church of S. Maria Nuova dates from the 13th century and has preserved two Gothic portals of that period. In the apse we can admire the beautiful 15th-century stalls.

We can continue as far as the Porta S. Antonio of 1374 and the 13th-century Church of S. Maria di Monteluce which was remodelled in the 14th century. The façade, which was remodelled in the 15th, has a 13th-century twin portal and a rose-window, and is flanked by a truncated campanile at the base of which a Renaissance chapel has been built. The single-interior has a marble tabernacle by Francisco di Simone Ferruci da Fiesole (1487).

Retracing our steps as far as Via Pinturicchio, we will find, at No. 7, the house where the painter lived and, at No. 1, an Etruscan cinerary urn. We reach Piazza Braccio Fortebraccio where we find the Palazzo Gallenga Stuart, a beautiful Baroque construction by Carattoti, and the so-called Arco di Augusto, the ancient city gate. The foundations date from the Etruscan period, but the upper part was rebuilt after the fire in 40 B.C.

We take Corso Garibaldi with, on the right, the Gothic Church of S. Agostino with its fine 16th-century stalls and, on the same *piazza*, the 15th-century Oratory of the Brotherhood with its Renaissance portal. Our next building, the Church of S. Angelo, was originally either a Roman temple dedicated to Christianity in the 5th and 6th centuries, or a late 5th-century church that was built with Roman material. This is a circular building whose central part, which is much higher, rests on a polygonal drum that is supported by 16 Classical Corinthian columns whose shafts are of different height and material. The church was originally in the form of a Greek cross, but of the four chapels only one remains, that of the apse. In the centre, the altar consists of a marble table resting on the drum of a column, which in Classical times was used as a milestone.

The Corso ends at the Porta S. Angelo, a massive crenel-lated tower which was once part of the mediaeval *enceinte* and rebuilt in 1326 by order of Braccio Fortebraccio.

We will come back to Piazza Braccio Fortebraccio and take Via S. Elisabetta where a Graeco-Roman building has a beautiful Roman mosaic of the early 2nd century A.D., depicting numerous animals.

We soon reach Piazza S. Francesco, a large space used by the Franciscans when they preached out-of-doors, with the large Church of S. Francesco of 1230—its façade was rebuilt after the ancient one—and the Oratory of San Bernardino with its magnificent polychrome façade by Agostino di Duccio (1457) in which both marble and terracotta are used. The exquisite bas-reliefs are also polychrome. This façade, one of the jewels of Perugia, is considered the artist's masterpiece.

The ancient Franciscan Convent, which is now the Academy of Fine Arts, is fronted by a Renaissance portico. Farther on, the Chapel of the Brotherhood of the Gonfalon (standard) of Saint Francis contains the standard and several tombs.

Via S. Francesco leads to the 15th-century House of the Knights of Malta and to the small Renaissance Church of la Madonna della Luce which was built by Giulio Danti and Rosetto with its elegant façade. On the left is the Arco di S. Luca, the ancient Etruscan gate.

We take Via dei Priori, one of the oldest and most charac-teristic streets in Perugia. It is bordered by 14th- and 15th-century houses, often with older ones, like the 12th-century Tower of the Sciri. The 17th-century Church of S. Teresa is alongside, and the Church of SS. Stefano e Valentino with its Gothic apsidiole and portals. Below lies a picturesque quarter. If we have time we can stroll as far as the Porta della Mandorla, an Etruscan gate which was remodelled in the 13th century.

3. URBINO, DUCAL PALACE.

There now remain the quarters to the south. Let us begin with the Porta di Marte, an Etruscan gate which dates from the 3rd and 2nd centuries B.C., and the strange underground city of the Baglioni which was discovered beneath the Rocca Paolina.

In 1436 when Malatesta Baglioni became Prince of Perugia, he built his palace on the site of the Casa dei Guidalotti which had been torn down in 1398. A century later, Pope Paul III built his celebrated fortress from the design by Antonio da Sangallo on the site of the Casa dei Baglioni and that of several churches and convents. But the demolishers limited themselves to destroying the upper part of the buildings and this material was used to fill up the streets. Later in the 1848 the populace demolished the fortress and archaeologists discovered buried beneath it the ancient street of the Baglioni which led to the powder magazine. All this is a curious glimpse of mediaeval Perugia.

The Church of S. Ercolano stands against the ancient wall on the site where the saint suffered martyrdom. This is a very original 13th-century building. Polygonal in plan, it is flanked by high arcades which are slightly tierspoint and crowned by blind arcades. The interior has stucco decoration and 17th-century frescoes. The high altar is resting on a Roman 6th-century sarcophagus.

Taking Corso Cavour we reach the Church of S. Domenico which was begun in 1305 in the Gothic style, but rebuilt by Maderno in the 17th century. The façade is bare and the exterior has remained Gothic together with the late 15th-century campanile.

In the interior we can see the fine Gothic tomb of Benedict XI, who died at Perugia in 1304; it is attributed to Giovanni Pisano but is more probably by Arnolfo di Cambio or Maitani. It consists of an aedicule which is resting on high twisted columns decorated with mosaics and containing a rich sarcophagus on which the Pope is reclining; two angels are drawing a curtain which reveals the papal figure. Above, *The Virgin and Child* is framed by Saint Benedict and Saint Dominic beneath canopies. Of interest also are a wonderful 15th-century stained-glass window, fine Renaissance stalls and 14th-century frescoes.

The ancient convent is now the Civic Museum which has a rich collection of Etruscan and Roman art as well as prehistoric works.

We reach the elegant Porta S. Pietro which consists of two gates, one of the 14th century, the other of the Renaissance, then the Church of S. Pietro which was built at the close of the 10th century. The graceful octagonal campanile of 1463 is by Giovanni di Betto and Pietro da Firenze. We enter a 17th-century courtyard with porticos and a rich 16th-century portal leads to the church which has three naves separated by 18 Classic Ionic columns which resemble those of the ancient basilicas of Rome. There are numerous works of art. The central nave is decorated with large paintings by Aliense, who was a pupil of Tintoretto. More interesting are the five half-figures of Perugino in the sacristy, for they are part of the altarpiece of *The Ascension*. The stalls, which are of marquetry, date from the Renaissance. In the refectory of the ancient convent there is a terracotta lavabo by Buglioni.

If we have time we can visit also the Romanesque-Gothic Church of S. Giuliana of 1253 with its 14th-century façade faced with white and red marble having geometrical designs. In the ancient convent there are two fine cloisters, one from the 13th century, the other from the 14th, the last named attributed to Gattaponi. The ancient chapter-house dates from the 13th century.

After visiting S. Pietro we leave Perugia by the Porta S. Constanzo beyond which we find, on the left, the Church of S. Constanzo. But it has been entirely rebuilt; only the 12th-century Romanesque portal is authentic.

We descend the slopes of the hill between olive groves and

fruit trees and at the end of five kilometres find the Sepolcro dei Volumni (the Tomb of the Volumni), which is part of the ancient Etruscan necropolis of Perugia discovered in 1840. It is a most interesting and handsome tomb, and I strongly recommend visiting it for a glimpse into the little-known world of Etruscan art. It dates from the second half of the 2nd century B.C.

A flight of steps leads to the entrance of the tomb which was hewn out of the tufa and we find ourselves in what resembles a Roman house. First the rectangular *atrium*, then the *tablinium* whose walls are decorated with two terracotta serpents, while on the vaulting there is a Gorgon. Along the walls, on ledges of tufa, are nine beautiful cinerary urns, the most important being that of a magistrate of the Volumni, as is indicated by an Etruscan inscription.

We cross the Tiber and enter the large plain which extends as far as Foligno and Spoleto, pass through Ospedalicchio, then see the hill of Assisi and at its foot the large cupola of Santa Maria degli Angeli.

ASSISI is a picturesque art town in the centre of Italy with several interesting buildings, but these would not have been heard of, but for the fact that this is the birthplace of St. Francis, to whom it mainly owes its fame. Memories of the Saint have often become monuments and it is fitting that we begin our visit at the Church of the Portiuncula which is hidden beneath a large cold, stiff building which Pope Pius V commissioned in 1569.

When we appreciate the life of poverty and self-abnegation which Saint Francis chose, we cannot think without pity or even anger of the huge sums that have been spent in erecting these buildings to his glory, whereas the money might have been devoted to the poor. The Portiuncula would be a more touching church if it stood in the midst of woods as it did when the Saint was alive. For he no longer had the use of the farm at Rivo Torto where he and his brethren took shelter.

The Benedictines of Monte Subasio allowed him this small chapel which was abandoned and falling into ruins. It was here that Santa Chiara, moved by the teaching of Saint Francis, joined him, cut her hair and donned a cowl. According to tradition, it was here also that Saint Francis was granted by Honorius III the "Portiuncula Indulgence" in July, 1216. It was here finally that he expressed the wish to receive the visit "of our sister Death". He was brought here at the end of September 1226 and died on 3rd October.

Naturally, no one was pleased with the church as it was and there was a universal desire to decorate it. The result was a modern pinnacle in the Gothic style, then in 1829 Overbeck painted on the façade a fresco which covered the one by Niccolo da Foligno. Other 15th-century frescoes can also be seen.

In the interior, we find the cell where Saint Francis died. It has been transformed into a chapel and decorated with frescoes by Spagna, a pupil of Perugino.

We can see the celebrated rose garden where the saint threw himself naked to avoid being tempted by the Devil and the wild roses at once lost their thorns. Alongside is the Chapel of the Roseto, then the Oratory of Saint Bonaventura above the grotto where Saint Francis slept when he was tempted by the Devil.

We can visit also the ancient convent only a part of which dates from the Saint's lifetime, for it was enlarged at the close of the 13th century and during the 14th. We see a small cloister and among the paintings a *Saint Francis*. According to tradition, it was painted on the plank on which the Saint died and where he appeared, thin and emaciated, in front of a carpet accompanied by two angels.

In the town of Assisi Etruscan and Roman memorials mingle with those of Saint Francis and his Order. We enter the town beneath the 14th-century crenellated Porta S. Francesco and, making a left turning, at once find ourselves in Piazza Inferiore di San Francesco which is surrounded by a 15th-century portico that was finished in the 16th century. From here there is a view of the Franciscan basilica with its tower, its entrance porch and the façade of the Upper Church.

As soon as Saint Francis was dead, it was decided to build a church as his burial place. Brother Elias designed a double basilica and actively pursued the work of building. In 1236 painters were busy decorating the interior with frescoes and in 1253 Innocent IV consecrated the unfinished edifice.

The façade of the Upper Church is simple and pure with its twin portal surmounted by a precious rose-window and a gable with an oculus. On the left side, we enter the Lower Church through a charming Gothic twin portal, and likewise surmounted by a delightful rose-window and fronted by a Renaissance porch which was added in 1487 by Francesco da Pietrasanta.

The Lower Church is a severe Romanesque building. The nave is divided into five bays by semicircular elliptical arcades which are supported by massive pillars. The first bay, which was enlarged in about 1300 and forms a kind of narthex, is more in keeping with the Gothic style.

The entire Lower Church is decorated with frescoes, but I will not enter into detail. The ones in the nave are the oldest, some having been mutilated when openings were made for chapels.

The most outstanding frescoes are those in the third chapel on the right, which are by Giotto and his pupils, those in the vaulting of the choir are by a pupil of Giotto, those in the right arm of the transept by Cimabue and his pupils, and those in the left arm by Pietro Lorenzetti. In a niche, on the left, in the third bay of the nave there is a *Crowning of the Virgin* by Giottino. The remarkable frescoes in the first chapel on the left are by the great Sienese painter, Simone Martini.

According to tradition, there existed an underground

church which had been walled-up and where the Saint stood in ecstasy. In 1818 excavations were made and the Saint's body was discovered in a stone coffin. A crypt was built in the neo-Classic style but subsequently given more restraint.

The Upper Church has a single nave of four bays with a transept and a polygonal apse. The French Gothic vaulting is resting on clusters of slender columns which are not at all related in style to the vaulting of the Lower Church. It is difficult to believe that the same architect is responsible for the two edifices. Indeed, the Upper Church may have had different vaulting, for there exists, above the present vaulting, large crossed arches which are rectangular in profile similar to those of the vaulting of the Lower Church. The change probably took place in 1253.

A gallery runs round beneath the windows of the nave and, in the transept, beneath trilobulate arches. As a whole, the building is slender, very light and luminous, creating a strong contrast to the severity of the Lower Church.

Here also the walls are decorated with frescoes which are too well known for me to discuss. Those in the apse and transept are by Cimabue and his pupils and probably date from about 1277. Their present condition is rather deplorable because of the use of lead monoxide. The large *Crucifixion* in the left transept is especially impressive.

The upper row, in the nave, is devoted to scenes from the Old and New Testaments which are attributed to artists of the School of Rome and partly to Cimabue and his pupils, including the young Giotto, Cavallini, Torriti, Rusuti, who also did the frescoes in the vaulting. The lower row, which is devoted to scenes from *The Life of Saint Francis*, is by Giotto and his pupils.

Of interest also are the fine stalls of the transept and the apse, the stained-glass windows, the treasure chamber and, in the convent, the large two-storey cloister which was built by Sixtus IV in 1476. I prefer what is known as the "small cloister", the ancient cemetery which with its cypress trees has something poetical about it. The cloister was rebuilt about the close of the 15th century and likewise is of two storeys, the lower one having semicircular arcades and the upper elliptical ones.

On leaving Piazza Inferiore let us glance at the Oratory of Saint Bernard of Siena, which dates from the first half of the 15th century, with its elegant Renaissance twin portal. We will follow Via S. Francesco, which is bordered by palaces and mediaeval houses, with, at No. 11, the Pilgrims' Oratory whose interior is decorated with interesting frescoes. At No. 3, the Portico del Monte Frumentario is an ancient hospital which was built in 1267. We pass beneath a 13th-century arch and follow Via del Seminario also bordered by ancient houses with, at No. 2, the entrance to the Museum and the Roman Forum. The Museum has been installed in the crypt of the Church of S. Nicolo, which has been demolished. We can admire architectural fragments, mutilated statues, cippi and urns. A corridor leads to the remains of the Forum with the foundation wall of the temple, the base of the tribunal, that of a tetrastyle portico, for everywhere in Assisi the Roman town appears beneath the mediaeval one. This mingling of two different periods is very striking when we reach the piazza and see rising before us, flanked by the high People's Tower which is square and crenellated, the Temple of Minerva absolutely intact, at least the exterior, for it was made into a church in the 16th century and in the following one dressed up in the Baroque style. Goethe greatly admired the Temple, especially since it was the first Classical monument he had seen. He at once observed that this hexastyle portico with six Corinthian columns seemed to be resting on pedestals. Goethe was right, for in order to compensate for the difference of level between the Temple and the Forum, the architect had cut the stylobate and inserted steps between the bases.

On the *piazza*, we can also see a beautiful fountain, the Palazzo dei Priori of 1337 which contains the Picture Gallery, and the 13th-century Palazzo del Capitano del Popolo.

We leave, on the right, the Chiesa Nuova (or New Church) of 1615, take Via S. Rufino which is bordered by ancient houses and reach the Cathedral with its beautiful Romanesque façade, flanked by a massive steeple, partly 11th century, having double twin windows.

The Cathedral itself, which dates from the 9th century, was enlarged about the middle of the 11th and remodelled in the 12th and 13th centuries.

The façade, which is divided into three horizontal zones, has a lower zone of the 12th century divided into squares and three portals which are flanked by lions and griffins. The rich ornamentation of the central portal with interesting animals has taken its inspiration from Classical art. On the tympanum there is a *Christ Enthroned Between the Sun and the Moon* with *The Virgin* at his right and *Saint Rufinus* to his left. On the tympanum of the right portal we can see peacocks drinking from a vase and, on that of the left, lions.

Above, consoles with male heads and those of animals support an elegant gallery from which emerge a wolf, a she-wolf and two calves. In the central part there are three rose-windows. The central one is supported by three personages who are perched on fantastic animals and framed by symbols of the Evangelists. The whole is topped by a triangular tympanum which was added at the close of the 13th century.

The interior, which has three naves separated by massive pillars, was unfortunately transformed by Alessi in 1571. We can see the baptismal fonts where Saint Francis, Saint Clara and Frederick II of Swabia were baptised, a triptych of 1740 by Niccolo Alunno and the Renaissance stalls of the choir. Taking a small door we can descend to the oratory where Saint Francis prayed before preaching in the cathedral.

We can see in addition a Roman cistern and an 11th-century crypt with three naves and an apse with its Roman sarcophagus which was used for the tomb of Saint Rufinus, and whose bas-reliefs portray Diana and Endymion.

We will take Via S. Maria delle Rose, one of the most characteristic streets in Assisi, with, at No. 2, the Palazzo dei Consoli, a 13th-century palace with two twin Romanesque windows. Passing the 13th-century Church of S. Maria delle Rose, we can ascend as far as the Rocca Maggiore where young Frederick II of Swabia stayed. In 1198 the people of Assisi destroyed part of the fortress. Rebuilt by Cardinal d'Albornoz about 1367, it was finished in 1458 by the construction of a polygonal tower and in 1535 by that of a massive cylindrical tower near the entrance. The fortress consists of a trapezoidal *enceinte* with angle towers and a massive square keep from which there is a wonderful view over the Umbrian plain and the Gorge of the Tescio.

We will return as far as Piazza del Duomo, then the 12th-century Porta Pertici. Taking Via del Comune Vecchio with its remains of mediaeval houses, we reach the ruins of the Roman Amphitheatre which dates from the early dates of the Empire, and those of the Roman Theatre, near the Cathedral, and finally the Church of Santa Clara, which is in imitation of the Upper Church of S. Francesco.

Those who have come to Assisi for its memories of Saint Francis should not fail to visit the Eremo delle Carceri and the rustic Church of S. Damiano.

Throughout his life Saint Francis remained attached to the hermit's love of nature and solitude. From the Porta dei Cappucini, a road leads to the Hermitage situated in a wild gorge with luxurious vegetation. A small oratory, where Saint Francis meditated, was completed by a convent built by Saint Bernardino of Siena. A low gate beneath a solid arch with a storey above, leads to a narrow courtyard with large flagstones, bordered on one side by the gorge of the torrent and, on the other, by the conventual buildings which consist of a refectory and several cells. The well in the centre of the courtyard is the one from which, according to tradition, water sprang forth after Saint Francis had prayed for it. At the far end, beneath a porch, we find the simple church which precedes the original tiny oratory. The sight is particularly moving with its reminders of that marvellous humility which characterised Saint Francis and his companions.

Beneath the sacristy is the Grotto of Saint Francis which consists of a cell and an oratory. It is now enclosed by buildings but originally stood in the open air. In the forest of green oaks there are other grottoes where the Franciscans lived.

The Porta Nuova leads also to the Church of S. Damiano. During Saint Francis's lifetime, it was merely a small rustic church which he himself repaired and where Saint Clara lived with other nuns. The façade has a portico. We can see the window from which Saint Clara faced the Saracens holding an ostensory and put them to flight.

The interior has great simplicity with its single nave and slightly tierspoint vaulting. We can visit the oratory which is decorated with frescoes, the garden of Saint Clara, the dormitory, the infirmary and, above all, the low infirmary with its groined vaulting where again the Franciscan spirit of poverty and humility is so striking.

The Porta Nuova leads to the Monastery of S. Angelo di Panzo which is now a farm, the church having been rebuilt in 1604 with the stones of the ancient building and, farther on, the Romanesque Abbey of S. Benedetto which, half-destroyed, was rebuilt in the 17th century. But we can still see a fine crypt with three naves dating from the first half of the 12th century and with transept and apse.

We will return to the main highway which now leads directly to the foot of the Subasio to SPELLO, an ancient Roman *municipium*, which has preserved its Porta Consolare, dating from Republican times and having three bays with, on the right, a high mediaeval tower.

Taking Via Consolare, where we can still see hanging on a wall the chain which was stretched across the road at night in order to isolate two quarters of the town, we reach the 12th-century Church of S. Maria Maggiore, which was remodelled in the 13th with a façade that was rebuilt in the 17th with ancient elements, and its Romanesque campanile.

The interior has a single nave which is bordered by lavish Baroque altars. On the left the Renaissance Baglioni Chapel has delightful frescoes by Pinturicchio who skilfully combined fantasy and reality, notably a graceful *Annunciation*. The same artist painted an *Angel* in the Chapel of the Sacrament which opens on to the left arm of the transept, and a delightful *Virgin and Child* in the chapel close by.

The Chapel of the Sepulchre contains a small museum with fine silver crosses and a *Virgin and Child* by Pinturicchio.

Farther on, we can see the 13th-century Church of S. Andrea with its simple Romanesque portal and, in the right arm of the transept, a large painting by Pinturicchio and Eusebio da S. Giorgio, *The Virgin and Child with Several Saints*. In the left nave, there is a *Resurrection of Christ* attributed to Pinturicchio.

Via Torri di Properzio leads to the Porta Venere, a fine construction from the time of Augustus, which owes its name to a Temple of Venus which once stood alongside. The two walls have three gates with an inner courtyard. The outer wall is flanked by two beautiful twelve-sided towers.

We return to Piazza della Repubblica with its very much remodelled Palazzo Comunale, then taking Via Garibaldi we reach the 12th-century Church of San Lorenzo which was subsequently remodelled. On the first pillar we can see an attractive late 15th-century tabernacle. Then in a picturesque quarter we discover the small Church of S.

Martino which dates from the 12th and 13th centuries, the Roman Arch known as that of the Capuchins, the gate which led to the acropolis now buried almost five feet beneath the ground, a fortress-tower dating from the time of Alboronoz and, on the summit, the Church of the Capuchins whose apse corresponds to the façade of S. Severino, with its 12th-century rose-window.

After passing beneath the Arch of the Capuchins, we descend as far as the Romanesque Gothic Church of Vallegloria and continue to the Arch of Augustus, a Roman gate with all the nobility of a triumphal arch.

Continuing to descend, we reach the Chiesa Tonda, a church in the form of a Greek cross with an octagonal cupola, which was built by Giovanni and Bartolino da Domodossola in 1517 with an elegant portal by Mosca da Terenzona.

Slightly retracing our steps and taking the road to Fontevecchia, we find, on the left, the interesting, small late 12th-century Romanesque Church of S. Claudio. The asymmetrical façade is very picturesque with its three portals, its twin windows and its steeple wall.

The interior, which has three naves, is pure yet with a curious asymmetry. The arcades progressively diminish in size to create the illusion of greater length; they are resting, on the right, on columns and, on the left, on pillars. The lateral naves are of unequal height. The altar consists of a pillar and the lid of a Roman sarcophagus. The walls are decorated with numerous frescoes, those of the apse are by Cola Petruccioli (1393).

Immediately on the right, we see the ruins of the Roman Amphitheatre which was 330 feet by 250, then, on the left, the Church of S. Maria del Mausoleo whose apse is supported by the ruins of a Roman tomb. We next pass beneath the spur which supports Spello with, above, the two towers of the Porta Venere from which descends the wall of Augustus.

We finally reach the beautiful Porta S. Ventura which likewise dates from the time of Augustus. It is well preserved and now walled-up.

On leaving the Porta Montanara, which is flanked by a mediaeval tower, we find also the Church of S. Girolamo of 1474, near the cemetery. It is fronted by an elegant Renaissance portico with Ionic columns and decorated with several frescoes dating from the 15th and 16th centuries.

We cross the Chiona and soon reach FOLIGNO on the left bank of the Topino.

The town suffered greatly during the last war and was rebuilt. It thus has a modern look, while preserving several interesting buildings, the most remarkable being the Cathedral which we find in the centre of the town.

The Cathedral was built in 1133, enlarged in 1201 and drastically transformed in the 16th and 18th centuries. The Romanesque façade has been over-restored, but on the nearby square we can see a wonderful lateral façade which was built by Masters Rodolfo and Binello in 1201. It has a magnificent richly decorated Romanesque portal with, on the arch mouldings, *The Symbols of the Evangelists*, *The Signs of the Zodiac* and a Cosmato mosaic decoration, while the inner side has casings and bas-reliefs representing *Frederick Barbarossa* and *Bishop Anselmo*. Above, a cornice resting on consoles with animal heads is surmounted by a loggia between two small rose-windows and by a large rose-window between twin windows.

The interior in the form of a Latin cross has a single nave and was rebuilt in the early 16th century by Cola da Caprarola from the design by Sangallo the Elder, but it was remodelled in the 18th century. Of the original building, there remains a crypt with reused columns which is rich in inscriptions on fragments from different periods.

On the two near-by *piazze* we can see several palaces, including the Palazzo Trinci which contains the Picture

Gallery and the Archaeological Museum. The palace has a
neo-Classic façade but really dates from the 14th and 15th
centuries. Several rooms on the second floor are beautifully
decorated with frescoes. After a vestibule whose walls are
decorated with 15th- and 16th-century frescoes and ornamental motifs, the wooden ceiling having the coat-of-arms of
Sixtus IV, we enter the loggia whose frescoes are in the style
of the Sanseverinati. Next is the chapel which was decorated
by Ottavio Nelli in 1424, followed by the Room of the Liberal
Arts and the Planets. Richly-dressed ladies seated on thrones
represent Grammar, Dialectics, Music, Geometry, Philo-
sophy, Astrology, Arithmetic and Rhetoric, while the
planets also are represented. These early 15th-century
frescoes are probably by a local Master who was influenced
by French miniaturists.

The same artist probably painted the large men in the
corridor, while the Room of Giants was painted by a pupil of
Nelli.

There are paintings in the other rooms, including a fresco
by Benozzo Gozzoli, *The Angel of the Annunciation.*

In the Church of S. Nicolo, which has a fine 16th-century
portal, we can admire two paintings by Niccolo Alunno who
was born at Foligno and a pupil of Benozzo Gozzoli. Alunno
is one of the masters of the Umbrian School whose work is
marked by great expression and passion. On the second altar,
on the right, there is a large polyptych by him and, at the far
end of the right nave, *The Coronation of the Virgin Between
Several Saints,* which is considered his masterpiece.

After the Cathedral, the most interesting building in
Foligno is the Church of S. Maria Intraportas which we find
on the huge Piazza S. Domenico where the church of the
same name has a handsome Gothic portal and a 14th-century
campanile.

S. Maria Intraportas does not have a prepossessing
appearance. Its façade is fronted by a portico of the 11th and

12th centuries set against four Roman columns. Flanking the
nave is a massive Romanesque column.

But the interior is not lacking in character. The three
naves are separated by pillars; the central one has barrel-
vaulting, the lateral naves, added in the 15th century, have
ogival vaulting. The walls are decorated with frescoes. In the
right nave, we can see three *Crucifixions*, the first attributed
to Mezzastris who did several saints on the pillars. But
the most interesting are at the entrance to the left nave in
the 12th-century Chapel of the Assumption. They have a
Byzantine character and date from the second half of the
12th century.

Taking the road to Camerino, we should not fail to see the
Benedictine ABBEY OF SASSOVIVO. We follow the N.77
for six kilometres as far as Uppello where a newly-constructed
road leads to the abbey.

The church has been rebuilt and decorated in an abomin-
able manner, but the Romanesque cloister is a real jewel.
An inscription and the date 1229 indicate that it was built by
Pietro Da Maria. It consists of 128 coupled columns, smooth
or spiral, which support semicircular arcades. Marble
statues of different colours and decorative mosaics create an
unusual graceful design. In 1314 Gothic terracotta blind
arcades were added at the side of the church. In the centre a
cistern of 1340 was remodelled in 1623.

We return to Foligno and take the road to Bevagna which
joins the N.75 shortly before reaching Foligno.

BEVAGNA is the ancient Umbrian *Mevania* which became
a prosperous Roman *municipium* praised by Strabo, Pliny,
Livy, Propertius and Tacitus. Destroyed by the barbarians
in the 6th century, it was burnt by Frederick Barbarossa in
1152 and again by Frederick II's army in 1249.

Just before entering the town, we can see, on the right, the
small Church of la Madonna della Rosa of 1469 and,
behind, the ruins of the Roman amphitheatre.

Numerous Roman ruins exist beneath the present town. The mediaeval ramparts were built from 1249 to 1377 on the foundation of the Roman *enceinte* which was flanked by square, polygonal or cylindrical towers and had five gates. Roman walls are quite distinguishable in different places, notably on the left of the Porta Flaminia and near the Porta Molini.

Entering Via Matteoti, we find, on the left, in the Silvestri property, the remains of a Roman building and, on the right, the Church of S. Vincenzo, which has been made into a cinema, with Roman fragments on the façade. Farther on, we discover the remains of the Roman Theatre on which houses have been built in a semicircle.

Turning into Via Garibaldi, we see, on the right, the remains of a Roman temple which probably dates from the 2nd century, then in Via Porta Guelfa, on the right, a fine Roman mosaic dating from the first century of the Empire. Designed in black and white, the mosaic represents a sea-horse guided by a triton, dolphins, octopuses and lobsters; the mosaic probably belonged to the Roman baths.

We reach the late 13th-century Church of S. Francesco with its façade of that period, but the interior was remodelled in the 18th century. We will be shown the stone on which Saint Francis preached to the birds of the Pian d'Arca.

Taking Via Matteotti, we can see also the Church of S. Margherita of 1271 which was entirely remodelled in 1640, and the ancient Church of S. Maria in Laurenzia with its graceful Romanesque portal, then in the Palazzo del Comune alongside, a beautiful silver 18th-century statue of Saint Vincent, the patron saint of Bevagna.

Next is the Church of S. Domenico with its 14th-century portal and on the mediaeval-looking Piazza della Libertà, the Consuls' Palace of 1270 with its outer flight of steps, its portico with two naves and its two storeys of twin windows, then the Church of S. Silvestro which, together with that of

. ASSISI, BASILICA.

16. FOLIGNO, CATHEDR

16

MONASTERY OF SASSOVIVO,
CLOISTERS.

18. CIVITA CASTELLANA, FORTRE

S. Michele which we will soon see, is the most beautiful church in Bevagna.

Begun in 1195 by Master Binello, as is indicated on an inscription on the right of the entrance, the church has a handsome portal with classic arch mouldings, surmounted by a rich window with three twin bays having twisted columns and a cornice with sculptured animals.

The interior, which is in the basilican plan with barrel-vaulting, has three naves separated by large arcades resting on columns with various forms of rustic capitals. The choir above the crypt has ogival vaulting.

To the right of the *piazza* is the Church of S. Michele, a late 12th-century or early 13th-century building which is the work of Masters Binello and Rodolfo as indicated on an inscription to the left of the entrance. The monumental façade has a handsome central portal whose sculptures have been inspired by Romanesque art. The portal is enclosed by a mosaic in the Cosmato style. Above the lateral portals there are two triple bays; a campanile rises above the right part with, on the first storey, a triple ogival bay.

The interior has three naves and was decorated in the 18th and 19th centuries. The crypt probably dates from the 8th century and likewise has been remodelled. The semi-circular apse is impressive.

We then take the road to MONTEFALCO which is known as "The Balcony of Umbria" because of its fine position.

This is a quiet town which has preserved its ramparts, its winding streets and several interesting churches.

We enter the town through the Porta S. Agostino which is set in a picturesque crenellated tower that was once part of the 14th-century *enceinte*. We pass several ancient buildings, like the Palazzo Scorzoni, which has preserved a room that was decorated in the 15th century, and reach the Gothic Church of S. Agostino of 1275 which was enlarged in the

14th century. The simple façade has an ogival portal and the single-nave interior with its timbered roof terminates in a polygonal apse. On the right side, arcades communicate with a lateral nave. The walls are decorated with frescoes, some only recently discovered, which date from the 14th, 15th and 16th centuries.

We then pass several palaces and reach the ancient Piazza dei Cavalieri which is almost circular in form. We can see the Oratory of S. Maria di Piazza and several palaces, including the Palazzo Comunale of 1270, which was subsequently remodelled, fronted by a 15th-century portico.

Taking the steep Vicolo degli Operari, we descend to the Porta S. Bartolomeo which is decorated with the coat-of-arms of Frederick II, and see the apse of the Church of S. Bartolomeo, dating from the 11th and 12th centuries, with remains of the original building. On the other side, the Church of S. Maria Maddalena, which was transformed in the 18th century, is decorated with 15th-century frescoes in the style of Alunno, while others of the 16th century are in the style of Spagna.

Continuing on the right, we follow the wall and after a cylindrical tower, we find the Church of S. Chiara which was built in the 13th and 14th centuries and rebuilt in the early 17th. However, the architects respected the Chapel of S. Croce which is entirely decorated with frescoes that were painted in 1333 by an Umbrian who was influenced by Giotto and Sienese artists.

The Clara for whom the church is named is a local saint, Chiara di Damiano da Montefalco, an Enclosed Augustinian nun (1268–1308).

In a small *piazza*, on the left, we see the 16th-century Church of S. Illuminata which is decorated with numerous frescoes, including a *Virgin and Child with Angels and Eight Saints* by Mezzastris, the others mostly by Francesco Melanzio (1487–1524).

But the finest frescoes at Montefalco are in the early
14th-century Church of S. Francesco with its Renaissance
portal.

The interior, with its large nave and timbered roof,
flanked on the right by a smaller nave from which it is
separated by ogival arches, terminates in three apses.

This church is a real museum of Umbrian painting.
There are works by Umbrian, Tuscan and Sienese Primi-
tives, by Mezzastris, Alunno, Melanzio and Spagna and an
Adoration of the Shepherds by Perugino. But the most outstand-
ing artist is Benozzo Gozzoli who decorated the first chapel
on the right with several *Saints* and two episodes from *The
Life of Saint Girolamo* and, in the central apse, scenes from
The Life of Saint Francis.

This work is considered Benozzo Gozzoli's masterpiece.
His style has much charm, vigour and a popular flavour all
admirably suited to the subject matter.

There are other frescoes by the same artist in a church
which stands beyond the Porta da Spoleto and which we will
visit on leaving the town, the Church of S. Fortunato. It was
built in the 5th century but rebuilt in 1446 and remodelled in
the 18th century. The façade is fronted by a 14th-century
portico which is supported by four ancient columns.

On the left of the portico is the Chapel of S. Francesco
which was decorated with frescoes by Tiberio d'Assisi in
1512. Beneath the arcade of the portico, in front of the
church portal, is a *Virgin and Child Between Several Saints and
Two Angels* by Benozzo Gozzoli.

The interior has a single nave and is rather simple. On the
right altar there is another fine fresco by the same artist,
Saint Fortunato, and other frescoes by him. On the second
altar, the lovely *Virgin and Child with Several Saints* is by
Melanzio.

On leaving Montefalco, we have the choice of two
itineraries: the one which returns to the N.3 at Trevi and

which I will be covering in a later volume, continuing to
Spoleto and Terni. The other passes by way of Todi and
rejoins the preceding one at Terni or Narni. It is the latter
that I am going to describe here.

We return to Osteria S. Marco and continue to Massa
Martana. The road descends with, on the right, Gualdo
Catteno standing on a hill between two torrents, still enclosed
by its mediaeval walls which are flanked by towers. We can
see a massive cylindrical tower of 1494 and a Gothic church
which has preserved several frescoes.

We cross an uneven countryside which is dominated by the
huge mass of Monte Martano, leaving, on the right,
Montecchio which also has preserved its ramparts. We then
descend to Massa Martana which has preserved the remains
of towers from its *enceinte*.

The road to Todi passes the charming Church of S. Pietro
which is surrounded by the cypress trees of the cemetery
then, at the end of three kilometres, we take the road, on the
right, which after two kilometres takes us to the Abbey of
SS. Fidenzio e Terenzio.

This abbey from the 12th century and the façade has a
Romanesque portal. In the interior, we can see a 13th-century
pulpit, a raised choir with an ancient altar and a crypt with
the remains of frescoes. Alongside, a crenellated tower has
been built with another twelve-sided tower as its base.

One kilometre away, we can see the 11th-century Church
of S. Illuminata which was built on the site of a more ancient
building of which traces remain. The frescoes in the interior
are of 1430.

We return to the road to Todi which soon rejoins the N.3
bis, the Via Tiberina, which, as we approach it, gives us a fine
view over the small town perched on its hill.

TODI is one of the most charming towns of Central Italy.
It has preserved part of its three *enceintes*, the Etruscan, the
Roman and the mediaeval one, each more extensive than the

other. It is mainly the mediaeval town we are going to discover.

We enter through the Porta Romana which was once part of the third *enceinte*. Immediately on the right we find the Renaissance Church of S. Filippo Benizzi which is composed by an octagon fronted by a nave with a Baroque portal.

We leave, on the left, the 14th-century Church of S. Nicolo with its handsome portal and a rich rose-window, then reach the Porta della Catena of the second *enceinte* with an ogival arch and eagle, the town's emblem, and finally the Porta Maria of the Etruscan *enceinte*, which is surmounted by an elegant loggia.

We pass the Fontana Cesia of 1606 and reach Piazza del Popolo, one of the finest mediaeval *piazze* in Italy, with its three crenellated palaces and, at the far end, fronted by a flight of steps, the façade of the Cathedral.

The Palazzo dei Priori which was begun in 1293 has preserved its mediaeval aspect in spite of the two storeys of windows which were added during the Renaissance. The palace is decorated with a bronze eagle of 1339 and flanked by a tower.

The Palazzo del Popolo in the Lombard style is of 1213. A ground floor with a portico is topped by several bays. The same is true of the adjoining Palazzo del Capitano, a late 13th-century building which is fronted by a flight of steps. We must admire the graceful trilobulate windows with small rose-windows and gables above them.

The Art Gallery has several fine paintings by Il Spagna and Bicci di Lorenzo.

The Cathedral, which was built on the site of a Temple of Apollo, was begun in the early 12th century by Masters from Como and remodelled in the 13th and 16th centuries. The façade has a large rose-window and two small ones and three portals, the central one having an acanthus leaf decoration. The lateral façade is decorated with blind arcades and slender columns, the apse being treated in a similar manner.

The interior has three naves which are separated by columns alternating with pillars. The raised choir has fine 16th-century stalls. Frescoes and various paintings can be seen in a small museum.

We reach the Church of S. Fortunato which also is worthy of a visit. This too is a Gothic church which was begun in 1292 and is fronted by two Roman lions which belonged to an earlier building. The unfinished façade has three tierspoint portals, the central one being of unusual richness, with its numerous arch mouldings supported by slender columns; the design resembles the Cathedral of Orvieto. It is framed by statues of *The Annunciation* in the style of Jacopo della Quercia. The mutilated portal on the left side dates from the early half of the 15th century.

The interior is narrow with three naves of equal height and ogival arcades resting on polystyle pillars. The vaulting is ogival and the apse polygonal.

In the right nave of the second chapel there is a fresco by Masolino da Panicale, *The Virgin and Child with Two Angels* and, in the choir, beautiful 16th-century stalls.

To the right side of the church is a Romanesque cloister with elliptical arcades and, surrounded by gardens, the remains of the *Rocca* which was destroyed in 1503.

We next reach the old market *piazza* where we will find four large niches of massive architecture with a Doric entablature which belonged to a basilica or a forum with, at its base, a fine mosaic in black and white. In Via Cesia the Fontana Scarnabecco with a portico and seven columns was built in 1241 at the expense of the *podestà* whose name it carries.

In the crypt is the tomb of Friar Jacopone, who died in 1306, the joyful poet and innocent disciple of Saint Francis, whose jokes and clever sayings are often repeated.

On leaving Todi, we pass the Church of S. Maria della Consolazione, which is isolated midway on the slope of the hill beyond the town.

This Renaissance building is entirely in the style of Bramante, and several architects must have collaborated. It is in the form of a Greek cross with three polygonal apses and a semicircular one. Each apse has two rows of Corinthian pilasters with delicately sculptured capitals and a central cupola that was finished a century later. The interior has great architectural purity with large statues of the Apostles in niches.

We now follow the road we took to come here for six kilometres and then continue to Narni.

We should not fail to visit ACQUASPARTA which is a watering place and is still surrounded by its mediaeval *enceinte* flanked by cylindrical towers.

The Palazzo Celsi is an impressive 16th-century palace which was probably built by Domenico Bianchi who was also the architect of the Church of Il Crocifisso at Todi. The palace numbered Galileo among its guests. We must admire, above all, its courtyard with its two-storey portico with a mezzanine above it, and its rooms decorated with frescoes dating from the time the palace was built.

The pride of the Palazzo Celsi is the elegant chapel which was built by Isabella Liviani in 1581 for the tomb of Prince Celsi.

We can visit also the Church of S. Francesco of 1290 with its 15th-century wooden *Christ on the Cross* and the remains of a cloister.

We continue to Narni taking the road which, on the right, heads directly to Sangemini, passing the ruins of *Carsulae*, a Roman town destroyed by the Goths in the 6th century.

We can see the remains of an amphitheatre, cisterns, different buildings and the Arch of S. Damiano, the town's north gate. Somewhat farther on after a section of the

Roman road, the Church of S. Damiano, fronted with a portico which was built of stones taken from the ruins, is decorated above the entrance door with a mediaeval bas-relief. The interior has two naves and an apse and is decorated with 14th- and 15th-century frescoes.

We reach SANGEMINI where we see the 15th-century Church of S. Francesco with its fine Gothic portal. The interior has a Gothic polygonal apse and the remains of 15th- and 17th-century frescoes.

The ancient mediaeval town has preserved a certain character with its picturesque Palazzo del Popolo and its 12th-century Church of S. Giovanni with its handsome Romanesque portal decorated with Cosmato mosaics.

At the end of three kilometres, we leave the road to Terni on the left and continue to Narni through an undulating and very populated countryside. We cross over two torrents by a Roman bridge which was partly destroyed during the last war and then rebuilt with salvaged material, then we see, to the right and to the left, the Roman tombs which were built along the Via Flaminia. Finally we reach NARNI on a hill covered with olive groves.

This town, which has preserved its mediaeval aspect, had great military importance from the time of the Umbrians and the Romans. It is the birthplace of Erasmus or Narni, surnamed Gattamelata, the celebrated *condottiere* of the Venetian Republic whose equestrian statue by Donatello can be seen at Padua.

We enter the town by the late 15th-century Porta Tenara which is flanked by massive towers, and reach Piazza Garibaldi where we see a mediaeval tower and the Romanesque Cathedral which was begun in 1145. Its façade, which faces another *piazza*, is fronted by an elegant 15th-century portico beneath which a handsome 12th-century portal is decorated in a very pure style. On the right, a delicately decorated arcade of 1497 leads to a chapel of the same period.

After the only Roman gate still existing, known as that of
the Bishop's Palace, and the two massive house-towers in
Via Caterina Frenceschi Ferrucci, we see the 15th-century
Church of S. Agostino and, on Piazza Priora, the Loggia dei
Priori which dates from the mid-14th century and is attributed
to Gattaponi, the Casa Sacripanti with its bas-reliefs and the
Palazza del Podestà consisting of three connecting 13th-
century buildings which were remodelled in the 16th century.
On the right of the entrance portal is a fine 13th-century
Romanesque bas-relief. We then enter an impressive vesti-
bule which is decorated with marble statues and inscriptions.
On the first floor, the Art Gallery has several fine works by
15th-century Sienese and Umbrian artists, notably a large
Coronation of the Virgin by Girlandaio and an *Annunciation* by
Benozzo Gozzoli.

At the far end of the *piazza* there is a lovely fountain of
1301 similar to the one we have admired at Perugia.

We will take Via Mazzini which leads to the Church of
S. Maria in Pensole of 1175, a Romanesque building fronted
by a portico which has a handsome portal decorated with
acanthus leaves.

The interior has three naves separated by Romanesque
columns with the remains of 14th-century frescoes and a crypt,
which is an earlier church that was buried in the 9th century.

We next find several 18th-century palaces, two towers of
the high Middle Ages and the half-ruined ancient Church of
S. Domenico with a fine 12th-century portal having a vegetal
décor, busts of the Apostles and, above, a cornice which is
supported by consoles decorated with masques and animal
heads. On the left is a massive campanile. In the interior are
frescoes, some dating from the 13th century.

Next we find a 12th-century house-tower. From the Garden
of S. Bernardo there is a wonderful view over the valley.

There are ancient houses in Via S. Bernardo and Via
Aurelio Saffi. The 14th-century Church of S. Francesco has a

rich Gothic portal with an aedicule above. From the *Rocca* also there is a fine view over the valley.

Taking the road to Terni, we can see before leaving the surroundings the 14th-century Church of S. Girolamo and the bridge over the Nera known as the Bridge of Augustus, a wonderful Roman work which was in ruins in the 7th or 8th century and restored with the addition of a new pier and two towers, then in ruins again in 1053. Originally it had four arcades.

The road follows the valley of the Nera, then crosses an uninhabited but well-cultivated countryside and we reach Otricoli, an ancient town surrounded by walls flanked by towers, with the remains of its fortress and the 13th-century Church of S. Maria which has been greatly remodelled.

The road descends rapidly and we soon see the 13th-century Castle of the Formiche whose crenellated walls and ruins stand on a kind of tufa base.

We cross the Aia and enter Latium. The road follows the Valley of the Tiber at the foot of hills and on one of them, some hundreds of yards away, is the lovely, ancient town of MAGLIANO SABINO.

We can visit the Cathedral which was rebuilt in 1735, the Church of S. Pietro with three naves separated by ten ancient columns, still much in the Romanesque style, and the Church of S. Michele.

The road crosses the Tiber and we reach CIVITA CASTELLANA which stands on the site of *Falerii Veteres*, the metropolis of the Falisci, which was captured by Camillus in 396 B.C. and destroyed by the Romans in 241 B.C. The inhabitants were removed to the near-by Roman *Falerium Novum* which we will shortly visit, but during the Barbarian invasions they returned to the site of their original town.

We are now going to visit two outstanding buildings, the Cathedral and the *Rocca*.

The Cathedral is Romanesque and there remains the

façade fronted by a wonderful portico, Ionic columns of antique imitation framing a large arcade. According to the inscription, the portico was built in 1210 by Laurentius Romanus, his son Jacobus and his grandson Cosma.

The façade has three portals. The handsome one in the centre is by Laurentius with a decoration in imitation of Roman mosaics; the one on the right has on the tympanum a mosaic with the bust of *Christ Blessing*. The one on the left is modern.

The interior, which has a single nave bordered by communicating chapels, was remodelled in the 18th century. The crypt was perhaps a pagan sanctuary.

Let us enter the sacristy in order to see two handsome marble pulpits which were once part of the iconostasis, with a decoration by the sons of Cosma II dating from the mid-13th century. 13th-century frescoes which once decorated the Romanesque building were recently discovered.

The street on the right of the church leads to the *Rocca* which has been used as a prison until recently but which will shortly be restored.

The *Rocca* was begun at the close of the 15th century by Alexander VI from the design by Antonio da Sangallo the Elder. Later Pope Julius II added a massive octagonal keep. This impressive pentagonal fortress was inhabited during the Renaissance by Cesare Borgia. There is a beautiful rectangular courtyard with three Renaissance gates and a large *cour d'honneur* with a double loggia decorated with frescoes by the School of the Zuccari.

Of interest also at No. 15 Corso Umberto is the Palazzo Trocchi with its fine courtyard, the small Church of S. Maria del Carmine with its delightful Romanesque campanile, its semicircular apse and its well-preserved interior with three naves. At the end of the Corso is a ruined Romanesque church with a fine portal.

We should not fail to visit the ruins of *Falerii* which

lie six kilometres away on the Fabrica di Roma road.

After crossing the Fosso Maggiore over the Terrano Bridge, we find the Etruscan necropolis whose burial chambers are fronted by a vestibule. But the ruins of *Falerium*, the Roman town which replaced the original *Falerii* in the 3rd century, lie several kilometres away, on the left, some 200 yards from the road.

The wall which enclosed the town still exists. It is trapezoidal in form, flanked by 50 towers and has nine gates which are relatively well preserved, offering an excellent idea of what a fortified Roman town was like. The best preserved gates are that of Jupiter and that of the Ox on the south angle, so called because of the head of an ox represented on the keystone. In the interior of the town, that is, in the midst of a field, we can see the remains of a theatre, a forum, a piscina and, above all, the remarkable ruins of the 12th-century Romanesque Church of S. Maria di Falleri.

The nave is in ruins, flanked by side-aisles likewise in ruins from which it is separated by pillars alternating with columns taken from Roman buildings. The semicircular apse is decorated, on the exterior, with blind arcades, every other one resting on a tall slender column. The apse is framed on each side by two apsidioles which are also decorated with blind arcades

We return to Civita Castellana where we take the road to NEPI which we enter after having crossed the Fosso di Fontanacupa. This is a picturesque town, once an Etruscan one, with, on its main *piazza*, a Palazzo Comunale which was begun by Vignola and finished in the Baroque taste.

We should not fail to see the fortress which was begun by Rodrigo Borgia. The *ensemble* is picturesque with its cylindrical keep, its ramparts, its towers and its bastions.

We can still see the town's mediaeval walls with fragments of the Etruscan one, the Church of S. Biagio with its Romanesque portal, and the Cathedral which was damaged by the

French in 1798, then rebuilt in 1831. From the Romanesque
period it has preserved a portico with three arcades and a
Lombard crypt.

Next we reach CASTEL S. ELIA which is but two kilometres away. It is not the town which interests us, but rather
the basilica which stands in a picturesque setting in a
solitary gorge. We can enter directly or through a modern
convent and a flight of steps.

According to tradition, the building was founded by Saint
Benedict in 520 and doubtless rebuilt in the 11th century.
The basilica is a remarkable Romanesque work with a
façade having three simple portals and an interior with three
naves which are separated by columns that once belonged to
ancient buildings. There is a timbered roof and the floor is
paved with the remains of mosaics. The pulpit dates from the
11th century and the high altar has a Cosmato decoration.
The transept and the apse are decorated with interesting
frescoes which date from the late 11th and early 12th century.

The cemetery on the right of the basilica is impressive with
its cypress trees and ancient columns.

We reach the Via Cassia which leads to Rome, but we can
make a final stop by taking, on the left, two kilometres before
Madonna di Bracciano, the road towards Isola Farnese in
order to see the ruins of VEII.

This important Etruscan town, once the rival of Rome,
was rich in luxurious palaces, impressive temples and
gigantic walls when Rome was little more than a collection
of mud huts. It was the Veientes who dictated the style of the
new city.

The first Roman attempt to liberate themselves from this
gentle yoke met with failure. Three hundred youths belonging to the Fabian family left to capture Veii, but they were
ambushed and all but one were massacred.

Veii lying on its rock was impregnable and it was besieged
in vain over the years. It was only after penetrating through

the sewers and canals that the Romans finally seized the town.

Following a desperate struggle only a handful of the population remained. Colonists were sent by Rome, but the town continued to decay and, during the reign of Augustus, Propertius mentioned the tragic destiny of this Etruscan town. "Oh, Veii! Yesterday you were a kingdom, a gold throne on your forum! But to-day only the horn of an indolent shepherd echoes within your walls and the bones of your inhabitants serve as fertilizer."

What do we now see? A huge deserted plateau, a peak overlooking ravines with rusty-coloured stones, galleries which are sinking into the mountain with murmuring streams which still fill the sacred founts.

After crossing the Fosso Mola which forms a cascade, we reach a well preserved part of the Roman Road. We pass by way of the Portonaccio and reach a terrace below the town where we find traces of the Roman Road on those of the Etruscan one, a large piscina, an Etruscan tunnel and the foundation of a temple known as that of Apollo, which supplied a great number of terracotta ex-votos, and the famous *Apollo* attributed to Vulca, the sole Etruscan sculptor whose name has come down to us and who executed the terracotta statues which once decorated the Temple of Jupiter on the Capitoline Hill at Rome. This statue, which dates from the close of the 6th century B.C. and is now in the museum of the Villa Giulia, is unusually realistic; hieratic and archaic qualities give much force to this cruel and malicious figure.

Returning to the Mola, we continue to the picturesque Isola Bridge, leaving on the left a tunnel more than 1,200 feet long which was used to divert water from the River Cremera. We will descend to the Formello Bridge and, following the Fosso di Formello, we will reach the Soso Bridge, a natural creation obtained by excavating the rock. A corridor in the

side of the small hill leads to the Campana Tomb of the
7th century B.C. The door consists of cut blocks of tufa stone
and is flanked by two small lions of hewn stone. The main
chamber which consists of four sepulchres has barrel-vaulting
of the same kind of stone. These frescoes are the most ancient
ones that have been found to date. In these fabulous hunting
scenes, the horses are portrayed half-brown and half-white
with blue spots, having wings and human heads.

We next reach the summit of the plateau with the *enceinte*
of the ancient acropolis 200 feet directly above the two
torrents which join and isolate the peak.

It was here that the Temple of Juno once stood. According
to legend, the Romans had dug almost to the very sanctuary
and arrived at the moment when the haruspex had predicted
that the war would be won by those who possessed the liver
of the victim which had just been sacrificed. The Roman
invaders seized the liver from the priest's hands and captured
the town.

We now take the road to Rome which passes through Posta
della Storta which in the 18th century was the last postal
relay. We leave, on the right, the 11th-century Spizzichino
Tower and somewhat farther on, the picturesque Casale
della Spizzichina, some parts of which also date from the
11th century.

We reach the outskirts of Rome and see, on the right, a
large sarcophagus which is known as The Tomb of Nero.
After returning to Via Flaminia, we enter the Eternal City
by the Porta del Popolo.

FROM FLORENCE
TO ROME
BY SIENA

FLORENCE

S.Appiano

Poggibonsi
Staggia
Monteriggioni

SIENNE

Asciano

Monte
Oliveto

Buonconvento
Montepulciano

Montalcino
Pienza

S.Antimo
S.Quirico
Chiusi

S. Salvatore

Piancastagnáio

Orvieto

Bolsena
Bomarzo

Montefiascone

VITERBE
Bagnáia

Soriano
Gallese

Vignanello

Caprarola

Ronciglione

Sutri

Capranica

Oriólo
Romano
Bracciano

ROME

n

21. CASTEL S. ELIA, INTERIOR OF BASILICA

ITINERARY VI

FROM FLORENCE TO ROME
BY WAY OF SIENA

Certosa di Val d'Ema — S. Appiano — Staggia — Monteriggioni — Abbadia a Isola — Siena — Asciano — Monte Oliveto — Buonconvento — Montalcino — Abbadia S. Antimo — S. Quirico d'Orcia — Pienza — Montepulciano — Chiusi — Abbadia S. Salvatore — Piancastagnaio — Bolsena — Orvieto — Bagnoregio — La Civita — Montefiascone — Viterbo — S. Maria della Quercia — Bagnaia — Bomarzo — Soriano — Gallese — Vignanello — Caprarola — Ronciglione — Sutri — Capranica — Bracciano.

WE leave Florence by way of the Porta Romana and at Gallozzo take the bridge over the Ema and see on its hill, surrounded by cypress trees and olive groves, the CERTOSA DI VAL D'EMA which was founded by Niccolo Acciaiuoli (1310–1366), the descendant of a noble family who became rich from dealing with steel. Grand Seneschal of the Kingdom of Naples, Duke of Amalfi and Athens, Niccolo Acciaiuoli decided in 1341 to establish near his native town a sanctuary worthy of perpetuating his memory. In 12 months the charterhouse and its outbuildings were finished.

A flight of steps leads to a huge courtyard enclosed by arcades in the centre of which rises the church, whose façade of the second half of the 16th century, already dressed up in the Baroque taste, was entirely remodelled in 1844. The interior, which has ogival vaulting, is divided into two sections: the choir for the laity and that of the monks, the last named of unusual wealth with its complex paving of coloured marble, its panelling, its stalls and its frescoes by Poccetti.

After the Chapel of S. Maria, which was founded in 1408 by Cardinal Angelo Acciajuoli and is in the form of a Greek cross having ogival vaulting, 14th-century paintings and 15th-century stained-glass windows, we descend to the underground church with its massive forms and squat pillars. We see the late 14th-century tomb of the Cardinal, with his statue showing him armed from head to foot, beneath a kind of tabernacle with Gothic arcades.

We must admire also the reclining statue of the Cardinal by a pupil of Donatello and three fine tombstones, with the bas-relief figures of the father, the sister and the son of the founder of the charterhouse.

We next visit the reception room with its 16th-century stained-glass windows and its terracottas in the style of the della Robbia, the refectory with its terracotta by Giovanni della Robbia, and the three cloisters. The first has two storeys, the second is enclosed by a simple row of arcades resting on granite columns. Then there is the large cloister with its cemetery and the cells of the Carthusians which are decorated with sixty-six terracotta medallions by Andrea and Giovanni della Robbia and frescoes by Pontormo.

We can see also the Chapel of the Chapter with its *Crucifixion* by Mariotto Albertinelli and a reclining statue of Francesco da San Gallo, the pharmacy and the *foresteria* which is reserved for strangers.

We return to the road to Siena and continue to S. CASCIANO IN VAL DI PESA where, on the left, we see the Church of La Misericordia, a 14th-century Tuscan-Gothic building, with a fine pulpit decorated with bas-reliefs by Balduccio, a wonderful *Crucifixion* by the great

Sienese painter, Simone Martini, and two panels of a triptych by Ugolino di Neri.

Farther on, BARBERINO VAL D'ELSA, standing on a height, has preserved its fortified *enceinte* with a gate and the Palazzo Pretorio which is decorated with coats-of-arms. Alongside, the apse of the church has been rebuilt in an unfortunate manner.

Soon afterwards, we can take the road on the right which leads to S. APPIANO where we find a church that is partly Pre-Romanesque having three apses. The three naves are separated by pillars or squat brick columns with Corinthian capitals. The large arcades date from the 12th century after the campanile had collapsed in 1171.

Fronting the church are the lovely trefoiled columns of a baptistery which was destroyed in 1805: they are topped by elegant capitals. The baptistery was in the form of an irregular polygon with three apsidioles.

We return to the N.2 and reach Poggibonsi which was considerably damaged during the last war. There is little to be seen with the exception of the Palazzo Pretorio with its crenellated tower and the remains of the Gothic building.

Just before reaching STAGGIA we will stop in order to see the remains of the impressive fortress with its two cylindrical towers. The town has preserved its walls with square and pentagonal towers. In the church there is a fine *Communion of Saint Mary the Egyptian* by Antonio Pollaiuolo.

Somewhat farther on, some 500 yards to the left of the road, is the picturesque old town of MONTERIGGIONI standing on a prominence. It has preserved intact its beautiful circular 13th-century *enceinte* which is flanked by 14 rectangular towers and mentioned by Dante in Canto XXXI of his *Inferno*.

From Monteriggioni we can see, three kilometres away, ABBADIA A ISOLA, a village which was created around an ancient Cistercian abbey founded in 1001 and took the name

"Isola" because of the marshes which surrounded the small summit on which it stood. The abbey had considerable influence during the 12th to 14th centuries, but declined in the 15th.

We cross the village and find the monastery on the left. After entering the courtyard, we see at the far end of the 12th-century church and its façade topped by blind arcades.

The interior in the basilican plan has three naves, which are separated by columns alternating with cruciform pillars, and a timbered roof. The three naves terminate in three apses. Excavations have disclosed near the choir the original church of 1001.

Among the paintings, we can see on the altar to the right a *Virgin and Child Enthroned* by a pupil of Duccio known as the Master of Abbadia a Isola; though this is perhaps an early work by Duccio. The altar has a handsome altar-piece of 1471 by Sano di Pietro and in the left nave there is a large fresco by Vincenzo Tamagni.

Of the ancient abbey there remain one of the galleries of the cloister, the sacristy and building where the abbot lived.

We return to the road to Siena which leaves, on the left, Stomennano, and enter woods of oaks and pine trees. The landscape gradually changes, for we are now in the midst of the Sienese hills which are silvery yellow and reddish ochre in colour.

We descend to Piano del Lago, a hollow surrounded by low wooded heights, and after Fontebecci we pass the Villa Mocenni and then the Palazzo dei Diavoli (or Turchi), a mediaeval brick construction which was enlarged by Antonio Federighi in 1460 by the addition of two buildings: on the right a projecting section with a curious cylindrical tower decorated with busts set in medallions, on the left a chapel of wonderful simplicity with, in the interior, a terra-cotta *Assumption* by the same Federighi.

The path on the left of the chapel leads to the Villa

Bargagli Petrucci which is attributed to Baldassare Peruzzi and has a picturesque terracotta portal.

We pass the *antiporto*, the town's forward defence beyond the Porta Camollia, and reach SIENA which is one of the most fascinating towns in Italy for the study of the art of the 13th–16th centuries. Not a few hours or several days but entire weeks can be spent here strolling in the narrow streets which intermingle around Piazza del Campo, the shell-shaped place that forms the heart of the town.

Siena has 60 churches, numerous palaces and museums. Her history is too long to relate in detail. After the death of Countess Mathilda in 1115, she succeeded in establishing her independence. The Sienese Alexander III led the struggle against the Emperor Frederick Barbarossa who besieged the town in vain in 1186. The power then passed into the hands of the Ghibellines who lost it nine years later. This was followed by internal strife, coalitions, battles and plagues alternating with periods of prosperity during the entire Middle Ages until the siege by Charles V in 1555. In spite of the heroic defence by Montluc and the Sienese, the town surrendered to the Medici.

Siena has two centres of attraction which we cannot resist: Piazza del Campo and the Cathedral, and it is here that we will begin our visit.

Piazza del Campo is one of the finest and most beautiful squares in all Italy. Designed in the form of a Greek or Roman theatre, it is a vast shell-like place entirely bordered by palaces of red brick with, placed in the position as if it were a scene on the stage, the Palazzo Pubblico with its beautiful windows of three bays, the whole topped by crenels. Alongside rises the tall, slender Torre del Mangia, 335 feet in height, one of the noblest towers in Italy, at the foot of which is the Cappella di Piazza, open like a loggia. The chapel was rebuilt during the Renaissance and decorated with frescoes by Il Sodoma which have been much restored.

The Palazzo Pubblico, like many of the buildings surrounding the square, dates from the 16th century and contains several masterpieces of Sienese painting, including the famous *Madonna and Child Under a Canopy Borne by Saints*, the equestrian portrait of *Guidoriccio da Togliano at the Siege of Montemassi* by Simone Martini, *Good and Bad Government* by Ambrogio Lorenzetti and paintings by Il Sodoma and Vecchietta. We can also admire the original bas-reliefs by Jacopo della Quercia for the monumental Fonte Gaia on Piazza del Campo, for what we now see on the fountain are copies.

Leaving the *piazza*, we take Via di Città and find the Merchants' Loggia, an elegant building in the transitional style built by Sano di Matteo in 1417, then farther on, at No. 89, the 14th-century Palazzo Chigi-Saracini with its beautiful curved façade and two storeys of triple bays. The courtyard is graceful, the interior having been remodelled during the Renaissance.

Then on the right, at No. 128, we see the Palazzo Piccolomini which was built in 1460 by Bernardo Rossellino for Catherine Piccolomini, the sister of Pius III, a fine example of Florentine Renaissance architecture with an embossed façade. At No. 130, the Palazzo Marsili of 1458 is still in the style of the 14th century. At No. 15, Via del Capitano, the Palace of the Captain of Justice has arcades and twin windows.

We reach Piazza del Duomo which is bordered, on the left, by various palaces and the Hospital of Santa Maria della Scala with its frescoes by Vecchietta and Domenico di Bartolo. These frame what is not only one of the most astonishing buildings in Tuscany but also one of the least attractive because of the excessive richness and profusion of its decoration. I refer, of course, to the Cathedral itself. The façade is all the more disconcerting, as it was greatly restored in the 19th century. It was begun in 1284 by Giovanni Pisano who is responsible for the lower part and also for an entire group of statues, the originals of which we can admire at the Opera del Duomo as they have been replaced by copies. The upper part in the Italian flowery Gothic style is of exaggerated preciosity and gives the impression of something faked.

The interior also is of exuberant richness which disheartens me. There is not a single blank space on which to rest the eye; everything has been designed to dazzle us, from the wonderful floor paving by 40 different artists, to the coffer cupola over the transept crossing. The walls and pillars consist of alternating black and white bands, the capitals are richly sculptured, the vaulting is painted blue with gold stars, medallions and busts of pontifical sovereigns. The apse is decorated with frescoes by Bocafumi, the choir with stained-glass windows by Duccio, and the chapels with stucco work and statues.

The pulpit by Nicola Pisano is a marvel of its kind. It is octagonal and entirely of white marble; it rests on nine columns decorated with statues and bas-reliefs, some supported by animals. The Renaissance Chapel of S. Giovanni and its statues was built by Giovanni di Stefano in 1482 and decorated with frescoes by Pinturicchio.

The Cathedral is flanked by an elegant campanile. To its right side, we can see the unfinished extension which was begun in 1339 and so designed as to have made the New Cathedral a huge building.

In the left side-aisle is the marvellous Piccolomini Library which was founded in 1495 by Cardinal Piccolomini (later Pius III) with its celebrated frescoes by Pinturicchio and his pupils. After admiring the lateral portal, we can visit the Opera del Duomo which has wonderful statues by Giovanni Pisano which once decorated the façade, and many fine Sienese paintings, notably the *Madonna and Child* by Duccio which once stood over the high altar, and the triptych by Pietro Lorenzetti devoted to *The Nativity of the Virgin.*

We then descend to the Baptistery of S. Giovanni which lies beneath the Cathedral. The white marble façade of 1382, which is set off by the use of several coloured marbles, has three portals and is very graceful.

The interior is decorated with frescoes by Vecchietta and contains splendid baptismal fonts by Jacopo della Quercia (1417) which are among the masterpieces of 15th-century sculpture. The sculptures and bas-reliefs are by different artists, including Donatello, Ghiberti and Jacopo della Quercia.

Opposite, the Palazzo del Magnifico of 1508 was built for Pandolfo Pietrucci, prince of Siena, known as "the Magnificent". It was decorated with famous frescoes which were removed in 1844 and are now, some in the Siena Museum, some in the National Gallery and others in American collections.

We reach Via di Città and take Via S. Pietro where we find the Palazzo Buonsignori, still in the Gothic style, the finest private palace in Siena. Its Picture Gallery should be visited for its collection of Sienese paintings. We begin with the Byzantine tradition of the 13th-century with Guido da Siena and his school, then Duccio, notably his *Madonna of he Franciscans*, the Master of S. Pietro Ovile whose *Assumption* resembles goldsmiths' work, and the Lorenzetti, especially two by Ambrogio, *Virgin and Child* and *The Annunciation*, and the panels which his brother Pietro painted for the Church of the Carmine.

Next we find paintings by Taddeo di Bartolo, Bartolo di Fredi, Luca di Tomme, Lippo Memmi, Bernardo Daddi, Giovanni di Paolo, Francesco di Giorgio, Lorenzo Monaco, Matteo di Giovanni, Sassetta and late Sienese painters, such as Neroccio di Landi, Vecchietta, Sano di Pietro, Il Sodoma and Beccafumi.

We now have a good idea of Siena and its wealth of art, but if we have time, we can visit numerous other interesting churches and palaces for which I must recommend you to the local guides.

We can, however, see the Château of Belcaro if we head for Arezzo. We leave Siena along Via S. Marco and the N.73 with, on the right, the cemetery, and we pass the huge Villa di Monasterio which has been made into a home of rest. This is an ancient Benedictine abbey surrounded by a huge park with an attractive cloister whose arcades are resting on brick columns with stone capitals. The church which has three naves contains several paintings, including one by Il Sodoma.

Next, the Château of Belcaro comes into sight against the line of undulating hills and we reach this by taking a road which makes numerous bends and curves. This castle dates from the close of the 12th century but it was restored and made into a villa by Baldassare Peruzzi, who built the palace, the loggia and the chapel. The castle was restored in the 19th century. There are frescoes by Peruzzi and ceilings by Matteo di Giovanni.

We return to the road to Arezzo which we leave somewhat farther on at Taverne d'Arbia in order to take the road on the right to Asciano which crosses a curious, uneven, chalky countryside.

ASCIANO which lies on a height near the Ombrone is a characteristic mediaeval town rich in works of art.

We first see the Church of S. Francesco, now a secularised building, in the Romanesque-Gothic style, having a single nave, a timbered roof and the remains of frescoes. The Collegiate Church is a beautiful 11th-century Romanesque work with a rose-window on its façade which also has a crowning of blind arcades. The interior, which likewise has a single nave and a timbered roof, terminates in three apsidioles. There are interesting frescoes.

The priest will take us on a visit of the Museum of Sacred Art which has been installed in the ancient Oratory of the

Compagnia di S. Croce. We can admire several fine paintings by the Sienese School, notably a polyptych by the youthful Matteo di Giovanni with its lively colours, an *Assumption* by Giovanni di Paolo, a *Saint Michael Slaying the Dragon*, *Two Saints* and a *Virgin and Child* by Ambrogio Lorenzetti, a *Nativity of the Virgin*, formerly attributed to Sassetta but the work of the Master of the Osservanza, an *Annunciation*, two polychrome wooden statues by Francesco di Valdambrino and a *Virgin and Child with the Donor* which is attributed to Barna.

Of interest also at Asciano are the Civic Tower, the Gothic Church of S. Agostino, and the Casa Corboli with its frescoes by a pupil of Ambrogio Lorenzetti.

We will continue to the MONASTERIO DI MONTE OLIVETO MAGGIORE which lies on a wooded hill in a solitary site.

The abbey was founded in 1313 by Bernardo Tolomei who abandoned the world and retired with two other Sienese nobles to this solitary setting. Others followed and the new monastery which abided by the rule of Saint Benedict was confirmed by Clement VI. In the 15th and 16th centuries it was a brilliant cultural centre.

In the midst of cypress trees and olive groves we see the huge pink coloured buildings. The entrance is like that of a fortified castle with a fixed bridge replacing the ancient drawbridge, and the gate, which is surmounted by a glazed terracotta representing *The Virgin and Child Crowned by Two Angels* by the school of Della Robbia, is defended by a massive tower with machicolation.

The church of 1400 has a Gothic façade. The interior with its single nave was decorated in the Baroque taste in the 18th century and has preserved its fine stalls of 1505 by Fra Giovanni da Vareno with its panelling of birds, architectural perspectives, tabernacles, musical instruments and Sienese monuments.

We can visit the convent which like the church was built in the 15th century, beginning with the large cloister which is decorated with a group of utterly remarkable frescoes by Luca Signorelli and Il Sodoma devoted to *The Life of Saint Benedict*. The first 19 frescoes are by Il Sodoma, then one by Riccio, nine by Signorelli, the remaining number by Il Sodoma, who portrayed himself full-face, dressed as a knight, in the third fresco, his hair falling to his shoulders and at his feet, his favourite animals, including the famous talking crow.

Several frescoes by Signorelli are truly remarkable and typical examples of his vigorous and dramatic style, while those by Il Sodoma are fascinating for the picturesque details, the naturalism and studied attitudes, and the gracious faces.

In the corridor which leads to the church we can admire other frescoes by Il Sodoma, including a *Christ Carrying His Cross*, which is one of his most moving masterpieces.

We next reach the central cloister which is enclosed by porticos resting on octagonal pillars with, on the left, the door to the small room where Il Sodoma has painted the portrait of the Friar cook. We reach the small cloister, which is architecturally similar, then the refectory which was decorated with frescoes by Paolo Novelli in 1670.

On the first floor we find the wonderful library with its panelling by Fra Giovanni da Verona and the pharmacy, then we descend and visit the chapter-house with its grisaille frescoes and a *Virgin and Child with Saints* which is attributed to Fra Antonio da Bologna. Alongside, the Chamber of Justice is decorated with a large fresco, *Adultery* by Riccio, and a chapel with 15th-century frescoes.

We take the road to Buonconvento with fine views over the valley of the Ombrone which is planted with vineyards and olive groves.

BUONCONVENTO is a picturesque town which has preserved its ancient walls built in the 14th century on the ruins of those demolished by the men of Perugia.

In the parish church which was rebuilt in the 18th century, we can see a fine *Virgin and Child and Several Saints* by Sano di Pietro and in a picture gallery several other interesting paintings. The Palazzo Pretorio is decorated with coats-of-arms and has a small tower.

We will now follow the N.2 for ten kilometres and at Torrenieri take the road to the right which follows the valley of the Asso, then slowly makes winding ascents to MONT-ALCINO, one of the most interesting towns in Tuscany and remarkable, above all, for its massive fortress which was built on the summit of the hill in 1361, using part of the 13th-century walls, including the S. Martino keep and the massive S. Giovanni Tower. The other towers and the pentagonal wall date from the 14th century.

We must admire the original way in which certain of the towers face the gorge and, likewise, the outer buttress added by the Medici in 1559.

We enter a huge courtyard with, on the left, a nave of the ancient basilica. Several rooms on the upper storeys are beautifully designed. In one of them we find the standard of the Sienese Republic.

If we take Via Ricasoli, we will see, at No. 44, a 15th-century palace with an inner courtyard having porticos and a loggia, then at No. 31, the ancient Augustinian Convent containing the Diocesan Museum of Sacred Art, which has several interesting paintings. Alongside, the large Romanesque-Gothic Church of S. Agostino of the 14th century has several frescoes of the same period. Dismissing the neo-Classic Cathedral, which was rebuilt in 1818, we reach Piazza del Popolo and find the 14th- and 15th-century loggia with its two Gothic arcades, and the 13th- and 14th-century Palazzo Comunale with its portico and high tower. A room used as a small museum contains not only paintings but 13th-century ceramics of local workmanship as well.

Of interest also is the Church of S. Egidio of 1325 which
has a single nave and timbered roof and Romanesque
capitals of an earlier church, the Hospital of S. Maria della
Croce with its museum and its 16th-century cloister.

A road which leaves the fortress takes us to ABBADIA
S. ANTIMO.

According to legend, the abbey was founded by Charlemagne in the early 9th century; it certainly existed in 813,
and soon became an important Benedictine abbey and
received rich donations from Louis the Pious, Lothair,
Berengar II, Adalbert and several popes. During the Middle
Ages, the abbot was one of the most powerful vassals of Sienese
territory and in 1202 fought against Siena. The decline of the
abbey began towards the close of the 13th century.

The church is a typical example of the French influence in
Italy. Indeed, we have the impression of being confronted
with a building in Auvergne or Languedoc. The architect
himself was probably French, as is witnessed by the plan and
elevation of the building and numerous details: the cornices
with modillions, the columns which decorated the exterior of
the apsidioles, the blind arcades with their archivolts with
saw-tooth decoration, the capitals of the ambulatory and the
slender angle columns of the ground floor of the campanile.

The nave is separated from the side-aisles by high columns
alternating every three with cruciform pillars. Above the
semicircular arcades elegant twin windows ensure light for
the tribunes over the side-aisles.

The capitals, almost all of alabaster, are wonderful;
notably, the one which represents *Daniel in the Lions' Den* by a
sculptor who was probably French.

The central nave has timbered vaulting, whereas the side-
aisles and the ambulatory have groined-vaulting with cross
ribs.

The semicircular apse is surrounded by an ambulatory on
to which three radiating chapels have been built, light being

ensured by a large twin window. Around the entire building there are tribunes which continue not only on the reverse side of the façade but along the side-aisles as well. Those on the right were made into dwellings in the 15th century.

There are several interesting works of art, including a fine Romanesque wooden *Christ on the Cross*; on an 11th-century capital the remains of ancient baptismal fonts which were destroyed during the last war; a Romanesque wooden *Virgin and Child*; and, in the crypt, an altar table consisting of a Roman tombstone with, above, a fresco attributed to Il Sodoma.

Taking a door on the right side of the church, beneath the sacristy, we descend to the crypt which belongs to an early construction dating from the 9th century. It has three small naves and two apses facing each other.

The walls of the church, inside as well as out, are faced with travertine, and the decorative parts are of alabaster, giving the walls a transparent luminosity with an extraordinary play of gold tones.

The simple façade crowned with blind arcades was fronted by a porch which has since disappeared. The Romanesque portal of the second half of the 13th century has been inspired by French art and is decorated with elegant sculptures. The 12th-century architrave bears the name of the architect, the monk Azzone, who was a member of the Luccan family of the Porcari.

Another portal on the right side dates from the 9th century. The jambs are decorated with curious geometrical motifs and the lintel with fantastic sculptured animals. A third portal, which dates from the 9th century, is on the left side and decorated with geometrical motifs. A square campanile has been built on to the left side of the church between the nave and the choir. It is in the Lombard style, is decorated with blind arcades and the topmost storey has twin windows. Finally, there are two curious bas-reliefs on the left side, a winged bull with a woman's head and a *Virgin and Child*.

Little remains of the monastic buildings, which have been made into a farm, with the exception of the well which stood in the centre of the cloister and the 9th-century triple bay of what was once the chapter-house.

We can return to Montalcino and the N.2 in order to see S. Quirico d'Orcia, Pienza, Montepulciano and other interesting places. But, if we wish to avoid this detour, we can travel along excellent minor roads to Abbadia San Salvatore.

After finding the N.2, we will head for S. QUIRICO D'ORCIA, a town which has retained part of its walls with the picturesque Porta dei Cappucini. (The Roman Gate was mined and destroyed during the last war.)

The most outstanding building is the Collegiate Church which is mentioned as early as the late 8th century. It was built in the Romanesque style at the close of the 12th century and remodelled in its present style in the 13th. The interior has a single nave with a fine painted ceiling followed by a transept and three apses. On the altar there is a triptych by Sano di Pietro and the wonderful panelled stalls are a late 15th-century work by Barili.

On the exterior, three wonderful portals are worthy of our attention. The one on the façade is Romanesque and dates from the 12th century. Monsters fighting each other are portrayed on the sculptures on the lintel. The arch mouldings are supported by tall slender columns framed by two clusters of four slender attached columns resting on lions. Above, we see an attractive rose-window.

The two other portals are on the right side. One also Romanesque, but of the second half of the 13th century, is attributed to Giovanni Pisano. Designed in the Lombard style, it is framed by two caryatids which are supported by columns. The other, much simpler, is of 1298, in the Romanesque style also but topped by a gable.

Of interest also are several rather plain palaces, at No. 38, Via Dante Alighieri, a simple 14th-century Sienese house where Saint Catherine is said to have lived, and at the end of the same street the small 12th-century Lombard Romanesque Church of Santa Maria with its massive portal on the left side and a semicircular apse which is crowned by blind arcades.

We will take the N.146 to Pienza which is less than ten kilometres away.

PIENZA is one of those towns which were created by an ambitious prince. In this case, the prince was Pope Pius II who was born here in 1405 in what was then a village known as Corsignano. Aeneas Sylvius Piccolomini decided to make his birthplace into a town worthy of the name ("town of Pius"). Work was begun in 1459 under the direction of the architect Bernardo Rossellino, and had greatly advanced three years later. To please the Pope, those close to him, including cardinals, followed his example. When the Pope died in 1464, the town was not finished, but it offered an *ensemble* of buildings with great unity of style.

Piazza Pio II in the centre of the town is truly remarkable with its attractive wells and the various palaces around the Cathedral which, with its apse overlooking the ravine, is still Gothic in plan, although the decoration is Renaissance. The façade has much restraint and vigour with three portals and a rose-window. It is shouldered by large pillars which are flanked by two storeys of columns.

The interior has three naves of equal height inspired by *hallenkirchen* which Pope Pius II had admired during his travels beyond the Alps, and separated by pillars already in the Renaissance style. The choir with its flat chevet is framed by chapels which join at the arms of the transept, forming an *ensemble* of radiating chapels.

There are several interesting paintings, notably, in the fourth chapel, an *Assumption of the Virgin* which is one of

3. ABBADIA S. ANTIMO, INTERIOR.

4. S. QUIRICO D'ORCIA, SIDE PORTAL
OF COLLEGIATE CHURCH.

MONTEPULCIANO, PALAZZO
COMUNALE.

26. ABBADIA SAN SALVATORE, CRY▌

Vecchietta's masterpieces. He has admirably portrayed the sweetness of expression of the Madonna and the beauty of the angels.

In the next chapel there is a *Virgin and Child Between Several Saints* by Sano di Pietro, fine Gothic stalls and an altar by Rossellino. We can admire also the lateral façade of the building and, in the crypt, the beautiful baptismal fonts by Rossellino.

The Canons' House, on the left, contains the Diocesan Museum of Sacred Art, including several interesting paintings, notably by Vecchietta, tapestries, goldsmiths' work copes and a 14th-century pluvial which was once stolen by a policeman.

Alongside, the Bishop's Palace is a remodelled Gothic building. Opposite, the Palazzo Comunale has an Ionic portico topped by a storey of fine twin windows. The palace is flanked by a crenellated tower.

The most outstanding palace in Pienza is the Palazzo Piccolomini on the right of the Cathedral, which is Rossellino's masterpiece inspired by the famous Rucellai Palace in Florence. This is an impressive square building in the rustic style. There are pilasters separating each bay and the bilobulate windows are most attractive. Around the building is a stone step and everywhere we can see the crescents of the House of Piccolomini.

The courtyard is bordered by porticos with Corinthian columns and communicates with a suspended garden on to which there opens a portico with a two-storey loggia above. Set against the wall is an octagonal well which is decorated with bas-reliefs.

In Via del Corso we find the 15th-century Palazzo Ammannati which was built by Giacomo Ammannati, the favourite of Pius II, the small palace of Cardinal Atrabense and the late 13th-century Church of S. Francesco with its 16th-century cloister.

On leaving Pienza, we should not fail to visit the parish
church of ancient CORSIGNANO which is less than a
kilometre away, for in my opinion this graceful small
Romanesque church is far more precious than the opulent
work of Pienza.

It dates from the 11th and 12th centuries and its façade,
which is flanked by a handsome round campanile decorated
with Lombard bands, has a wonderful portal, the arch
mouldings decorated with a tooth design. The jambs have
arabesques and support a lintel which is decorated with a
siren. The attractive twin window above has a feminine
statuette which replaces a column. On the right side,
another portal has richly decorated jambs and lintel. We
can see a *Ride of the Magi, The Annunciation to the Shepherds,
The Adoration of the Shepherds* and very Byzantine fantastic
animals.

The interior has three naves separated by massive pillars
which receive the thrust of the unequal arcades. There is no
apse and the roof is a timbered one.

We head for Montepulciano, leaving on the left the
Castle of Bibbiano Cacciaconti which is surmounted by a
massive rectangular tower. We cross a pleasant countryside,
the hills covered with fruit orchards or wheat fields.

At the foot of the hill on which lies the town of Montepulciano, we find, on the left, the wonderful Renaissance
Church of S. Biagio which was begun in 1518 from the design
by Antonio di Sangallo the Elder and finished in 1545.
For architects, this church represents what Classical antiquity
has most contributed to the Renaissance period: clear design,
full composition and restraint in detail. Entirely built of
travertine which time has enriched with a lovely gilt patina,
the church is in the form of a Greek cross with a central
cupola and a semicircular apse. The façade, which faces
north, is flanked by two isolated campaniles. The right one is
unfinished, the left one has four different orders of columns,

superimposed, Doric, Ionic, Corinthian and Composite,
while the last octagonal storey is surmounted by a pyramid.
The interior is harmonious, admirably balanced and of great
simplicity.

Alongside, the Canonica is a posthumous work of Sangallo.
It has much elegance with its Doric portico surmounted by a
loggia having Ionic slender columns.

MONTEPULCIANO is the birthplace of the scholar and
poet Angelo Ambrogini (1454–1494). The town has partly
preserved its Renaissance character and the long street leading to the summit of the hill is bordered by interesting palaces
and houses. In a way, this is the town of Antonio di Sangallo
the Elder, as Vicenza is that of Palladio. For, while directing
the work at S. Biagio, Sangallo was requested by the town's
nobles to design several palaces.

On a large *piazza* outside the mediaeval walls, we see the
Church of S. Agnese of 1311. It has been greatly remodelled.
With the exception of the 14th-century portal the façade is
modern.

We pass the massive bastions of the fortress which was
built by Sangallo the Elder, enter the town beneath the
Porta al Prato and take Via Roma. Immediately on the right,
at No. 39, we find the Casa Ridolfi, the house where
Margherita da Cortona stayed before her conversion, and at
No. 37, the handsome Renaissance Palazzo Avignonesi
which is attributed to Vignola. Then at No. 33 the Renaissance Palazzo Batignani, at No. 28 the grandiose Palazzo
Cocconi which is attributed to Antonio di Sangallo the Elder
and at No. 29, the Palazzo Buccelli with Etruscan urn-
reliefs and inscriptions built into the wall.

We reach the Gothic-Renaissance Church of S. Agostino
with its curious façade in the late Florentine Gothic style by
Michelozzo. It is decorated with fluted pilasters and niches.
On the tympanum there is a terracotta by Michelozzo
representing *The Virgin Between Saint John the Baptist and Saint*

Augustine. The single-nave interior was remodelled in the 13th century.

Opposite the church stands the Pulcinella Tower. We then see in turn at No. 12, the Palazzo Tarugi Cappelli whose vestibule is decorated with frescoes by Zuccari, at No. 6, the Palazzo Venturi and then the Loggia del Mercato. The street becomes Via Cavour and at No. 9 we find the handsome Palazzo Cervini which was built by Antonio di Sangallo the Elder with an embossed ground floor, at No. 21, the Palazzo Gagnoni by Vignola, followed by the Church of the Gesù, with its elegant round Baroque interior, begun by Arrigoni in the 17th century.

If we follow Via del Poliziano, we will find, at No. 1, the 17th-century Palazzo Angelotti. A street leads to the 14th-century Church of S. Maria dei Servi with its Gothic façade.

We can ignore the ancient fortress which was entirely rebuilt, pass the Palazzo Bellarmino where Cardinal Bellarmine—who condemned Galileo as a heretic—was born in 1542, and reach the *piazza* at the highest part of the town around which are the most important buildings.

The Cathedral was built from 1592 to 1630 and the unfinished façade is flanked by a campanile of an earlier church. The interior contains several fine works of art, including the recumbent statue of Bartolomeo Aragazzi, secretary of Pope Martin V, which was part of a tomb by Michelozzo, and behind the altar, a wonderful triptych, *Death*, *Assumption and The Coronation of the Madonna*, by Taddeo di Bartolo (1403).

On the left of the Cathedral, the Palazzo Comunale is a severe late 14th-century building with three storeys having crenels, dominated by a tower which also is crenellated.

Opposite, the Palazzo Contucci, at No. 6, was begun in 1519 by Sangallo the Elder and finished by Peruzzi. It has a fine storey of windows framed by Ionic columns, surmounted by another storey which is Baroque.

Opposite the Cathedral, at No. 3, the Palazzo Tarugi is an original work by Sangallo the Elder in spite of (or because of) his errors: for instance, the much too long Ionic columns which are resting on exaggerated pedestals. In fact, the palace was subsequently remodelled and the upper loggia has been closed.

At No. 12, Via Ricci, we find the Palazzo Ricci de Peruzzi and at No. 11, the Palazzo Neri Orselli Bombagli, a Sienese Gothic building which now contains the Civic Museum, including works by Il Sodoma, Margaritone of Arezzo, Girolamo di Benvenuto and Spinello Aretino.

We next pass the 13th-century Church of S. Francesco with its Gothic portal, and the Church of S. Lucia with its Baroque façade, and finally return to the Porta al Prato.

We will take the road which passes through Chianciano which has preserved an ancient gate, the Castle of Counts Manenti and the 13th-century Palazzo del Podestà, then two kilometres away, through Chianciano Terme, which is a popular watering place.

Soon we reach CHIUSI which is mostly interesting for its Etruscan Museum and various tombs in the surrounding area.

The town enjoyed a period of splendour in the 7th and 6th centuries B.C., notably during the reign of Lars Porsenna, who captured Rome in 520 B.C. Chiusi was then known as *Camars* and later *Clusium* when the inhabitants became Roman citizens. The town was taken by the Goths, by Totila and then later by the Lombards, who founded a duchy there. About the 11th century, the town was fearfully devastated by malaria, and it was only in later times, after the Val di Chiana had been drained, that it recovered from the disaster.

Chiusi has preserved the plan of a Roman camp with the *decumanus* which corresponds with the second part of Via Porsenna and Via Arunte, while the *cardo* is followed by the first part of Via Porsenna, Via Baldetti and Via Lavinia. Beneath the town extends a labyrinth of subterranean passages which date from the Etruscan period, some being used as cellars for private buildings.

On Piazza del Duomo in the centre of the town, we see the Cathedral which dates from the 6th century. It was rebuilt in the 12th and remodelled in the 19th. The façade, which is fronted by a Doric portico, is flanked by a massive 12th-century campanile beneath which we reach a large piscina, probably from the 1st century A.D., having two naves and dug into the tufa stone.

The interior of the Cathedral, which has three naves separated by 18 columns of different styles all taken from Roman buildings, has a timbered roof and terminates in three apses. On the right, a column has the symbol of the Synagogue and an inscription mentions a gift of Duke Gregory and of his mother Austrogonde. On the left, another column has the symbol of the Church. In the chapter-house we can see 22 miniature antiphonaries of the 15th century from the Monastery of Monte Oliveto Maggiore. They are attributed to such artists as Rosselli di Bindo, Sano di Pietro, Girolamo Bembo, Andrea Mercati and Fra. Bartolomeo da Ferrara.

On the left, the Archaeological Museum contains a valuable collection of objects found around Chiusi. Indeed, this is one of the most important collections of Etruscan objects in Italy.

Of interest also at Chiusi is the 13th-century Church of S. Maria delle Morte and that of S. Francesco of the same period, and the 12th-century fortress of which there remains an outer wall.

The Etruscan tombs situated in isolated hills at some distance from the town are the great attraction of Chiusi. The landscape is typically Florentine with green slopes dotted with copses and large farms surrounded by vineyards, the roofs often having Etruscan funerary urns and sarcophagi used as drinking-water troughs.

We can now proceed directly to Orvieto which is but 50 kilometres away, or make a detour by way of Abbadia S. Salvatore which means an additional 40 kilometres.

We will take the road to Chianciano and soon leave it for the one to SARTEANO whose ancient town has preserved part of its mediaeval character.

We see the 14th-century Church of S. Francesco with its elegant 15th-century Renaissance façade flanked by a campanile of the same period, also the cloister, several more or less mutilated palaces, and the Church of S. Lorenzo of 1576, which was built with huge blocks of travertine taken from Etruscan and Roman buildings of the ancient *Pagus Sartheanensis*.

The landscape then becomes strangely solitary with, in the distance, the Fortress of Radicofani. We descend towards the valley of the Orcia, then ascend to discover a fine panoramic view of the countryside surrounding Radicofani.

We reach the Via Cassia and then RADICOFANI, built on the slopes of a basaltic rock crowned by the ruins of a castle which dates from the 13th century, but was rebuilt in the 16th and destroyed in the 18th.

The town has preserved its mediaeval character with its low stone houses having an outer flight of steps.

In the centre of the town, fronting a *piazza*, the Church of S. Pietro is a 13th-century Romanesque building whose simple façade has a portal and a twin window. To its left, the church is surmounted by a quadrangular campanile.

The Gothic interior has three naves and three apses.

Of interest also are several palaces and the Church of S. Agata with its Gothic façade.

We follow the Via Cassia for six kilometres in the direction of S. Quirico d'Orcia, then take the road on the left to Abbadia S. Salvatore which gives us fine views over the various neighbouring valleys.

ABBADIA S. SALVATORE, which has become a holiday

centre, owes its name to the celebrated abbey which was founded in 743 under the Lombard Rachis and soon became the richest one in Tuscany. It was first occupied by the Benedictines, then for a short time by the Camaldulians, and finally by the Cistercians.

The church was rebuilt in the Romanesque style in 1036, the sacristy dates from the 14th century and the cloister from the 16th. The interior was remodelled in 1590.

The high and narrow façade is restrained and almost bare; above a semicircular portal there is a triple bay and the church is flanked by two towers, one unfinished.

The interior, with a single nave having a raised choir and a timbered roof, has, on the high altar, a handsome wooden *Christ* which dates from the second half of the 12th century. The stalls date from the 15th century and the frescoes are by Nasini.

But the great interest of the church lies in its crypt, which is probably the original 8th-century church. It is now partly underground. In the form of a Latin cross, it extends not only beneath the transept but beyond it. The vaulting, reinforced by cross ribs, is resting on abaci, sculptured accordingly. The 40 columns, like the capitals, are all very different in shape, for example, one of the capitals has lotus foliage.

The mediaeval town has preserved its mountain-like character with its Gothic and Renaissance houses of black stone. Several palaces have unfortunately been remodelled and the Palazzo Comunale dates from the 15th century.

We should not fail to visit Monte Amiata which is one of the most astonishing natural beauties of Tuscany. The mountain is a large conical volcano whose highest slopes are covered with wonderful chestnut trees. It is rich in quick-silver mines.

There are good roads in the forests. If we have time, we can continue as far as Arcidosso and S. Fiora. In any case, we will leave by way of PIANCASTAGNAIO which lies at the edge of chestnut forests and overlooks the valley of the Paglia.

We enter the town beneath a crenellated gate on the left of the massive *Rocca* which belonged to the Aldobrandeschi and the Sienese. From the *piazza* its appearance is most impressive with its powerful keep, its heavy bastion and its tower entirely crowned by machicolation.

Of interest also is the large Palazzo del Marchese with its elegant staircase and the old Palazzo Pretorio.

We will take the road down to the valley with its wonderful view of the surrounding countryside. The N.2 descends the valley of the Paglia and passes through ACQUAPEN-DENTE where the cathedral is a Benedictine church that was remodelled in the Baroque taste in the 18th century. Opposite, the clock-tower is the remains of the fortress.

At S. LORENZO NUOVO there is a fine view of Lake Bolsena. The town was built in 1775 by Pope Pius VI to house the inhabitants of S. Lorenzo Vecchio, which was decimated by malaria. This is an excellent example of 18th-century urbanism with the streets intersecting at right angles and in the centre a large octagonal square.

We soon reach the shore of the lake and follow it to Bolsena.

Alongside the new town, which lies on the lake, Bolsena has preserved its mediaeval part and its fortress.

We first see the 11th-century Church of S. Christina which is fronted by an elegant Renaissance façade that was built in 1492 by Giovanni de Medici, the future Leo X. The façade of a 15th-century oratory has been built on to it and, on the other side, a campanile.

The interior has three naves separated by columns with a timbered roof and three apses. In the left nave, we see a wooden 15th-century *Christ on the Cross* and in the right nave, the Chapel of the Rosary whose walls are decorated with frescoes by 15th-century Sienese painters. The right apse also has frescoes of the same period. In the central apse there is a polyptych by Sano di Pietro.

In the left nave, a 12th-century door with a bas-relief representing *The Wise Virgins* and *The Epiphany*, leads to the Miracle Chapel where on the altar we can see a venerated marble statue stained with blood. The Miracle of Bolsena, the subject of a celebrated fresco by Raphael in the Vatican, occurred in 1263. Sceptical about the doctrine of transubstantiation, a Bohemian priest on his way to Rome was convinced of its truth by the miraculous appearance of drops of blood on the host which he had just consecrated. In commemoration of this, Pope Urban IV, to whom the host had been brought as he was staying at Orvieto at the time, instituted the festival of Corpus Domini in 1264.

We next enter the Grotto of Saint Christina hewn in the rock which was part of the Catacombs of Saint Christina after having been dedicated to the worship of Apollo.

On the right, we see the Chapel of Saint Michael at the entrance to the catacombs and, in the grotto, the altar of Saint Christina with a fine 9th-century ciborium. A basaltic stone, showing the implant of two feet, is said to be the one which was attached to the neck of the saintly daughter of the prefect Urban, who aided her and brought her safe and sound to the shore of the lake, into which she had been thrown and left to drown in 292.

We cross the ancient mediaeval town and reach the castle which dates from the 12th century and is very picturesque with its four angle towers, its fortified gate and its well-preserved courtyard.

We take the road to Orvieto with its fine views over the lake, then across a landscape covered with vineyards which produce the famous white Orvieto wine.

ORVIETO stands on an isolated rocky plateau in the midst of the Paglia Valley. Its strategic importance was recognised by the Etruscans who, on the site of the present cathedral, undoubtedly built their temples dedicated to the god of the seasons and fertility, Veltha or Voltumna, and to Nortia, the goddess of fate. Each year the leaders of the Etruscan towns gathered here to sacrifice to the gods and take decisions concerning the nation's political and religious unity. A great market was held, also festivities and games.

The Etruscan town was destroyed in 265 B.C. and the site remained uninhabited for two centuries. It was not until the 1st century A.D. that the place was occupied by the Romans. The new town was called *Urbs Vetus*, which later became Orvieto. The Goths settled here but were driven out by Belisarius. In 596 the town was occupied by the Lombard Agiluf. In the 11th century it was formed into a commune and many house-towers were built. This was followed by the usual struggles characteristic of such Italian towns.

The Cathedral of Orvieto is a first-class monument and there are other equally interesting edifices, but before visiting them let us devote our attention to the remaining Etruscan ruins.

We enter Orvieto beneath the Porta Romana with its remains of the ancient Porta Pertusa, then we reach Piazza della Repubblica which occupies the site of the ancient Etruscan forum. It is bordered by the Palazzo del Comune which dates from 1216 but was rebuilt by Scalza in 1573 with a series of arcades, a storey of large windows and a mezzanine; and by the Church of S. Andrea which dates from the 6th century, but was remodelled in the 11th and 12th centuries, then finished in the 14th and 16th. The façade with its 15th-century Gothic portal is flanked by a massive, crenellated campanile of the 11th and 12th centuries, having 12 sides with three storeys of twin windows. The form is similar to that of the Abbey of SS. Severo e Martirio which we will shortly visit.

The interior is in the basilican plan and has three naves separated by eight monolithic granite columns which seem to date from the second century A.D. The capitals are of the restoration of 1512. The roof is timbered and a double transept has 14th-century ogival vaulting.

The left nave, which communicates with the Church of S. Bartolomeo, has remains of 14th- and 15th-century frescoes. In the transept crossing we can admire the pulpit formed of ancient elements and 12th- and 13th-century Cosmato decorations.

The verger will show us the buried remains of the original basilica with fragments of choir-screen panels and 6th-century geometrical mosaic flooring, then lower down, underground sections of the Etruscan town, including a street, tombs, wells and the ruins of buildings.

Let us take Via Cavour, the principal street in Orvieto, which passes the Moor's Tower, then Via del Duomo which has a fine palace whose rich portal is by Scalza.

The Cathedral which stands isolated from all other buildings is one of the finest achievements of Gothic art in Italy. Its façade is incredibly rich with its lavish polychrome sculpture and mosaic.

It was after the famous Miracle of Bolsena, which I have already related, that Pope Nicolas V decided to erect a church worthy of containing the miraculous host, and the work was entrusted to Friar Bevignate of Perugia, who built it on the site of the Church of S. Costanzo which itself had replaced an Etruscan temple. The original design was that of a Roman basilica with three naves and a semicircular apse. In 1300 Bevignate was replaced by Giovanni di Uguccione of Orvieto who followed the designs of Maitani and continued the work in the Gothic style by covering the finished part with ogival vaulting, shoring up the walls with outer rampant arcades and making the interior also in the Gothic style, rebuilding the apse on a rectangular plan and putting the façade into commission. Although other architects, the Nuti, the Pisano, Orcagna, Federighi, worked on the Cathedral, the unity was not affected.

The façade is one of the most important examples of Gothic sculpture in Italy. Although it was begun in 1310 under the supervision of and according to the plans of Lorenzo Maitani of Siena, its upper part was not finished until the 16th century. Sienese and Pisan artists, among whom we can count Vitale, and Nicolo and Meo Nuti, assisted Maitani, creating a delightful cycle of Biblical scenes on the first two pillars, while the third has scenes from the New Testament and the fourth is devoted to the Last Judgment.

The large rose-window above is by Orcagna. The mosaics date from different periods, some having been remodelled or restored.

The lateral façades of alternating black and white stone have attractive Pisan portals.

The interior also is decorated with black and white bands. The columns have rich capitals which support semicircular arcades. We can next see the attractive Gothic baptismal fonts by the Sienese, Luca di Giovanni; then, in the left arm of the Cappella Nuova (New Chapel), the famous frescoes by Luca Signorelli. Fra Angelico was asked to work in the Cathedral in 1447 and, with the aid of Benozzo Gozzoli and other painters, he began to decorate the vaulting above the choir. But he was soon recalled to Rome. Yet, during the course of three months, he executed two panels portraying *Christ in Glory as Judge* and *The Prophets* to the right.

Then in 1499 Luca Signorelli was commissioned to finish the decoration and spent six years at the task. These paintings are not only the chief attraction here but also his most representative work. We must admire, above all, the two large compositions of *The Overthrow of Antichrist*, who is represented in the foreground preaching; according to tradition the two devout figures, in the corner to the left, are portraits of Signorelli and Fra Angelico.

We then enter the Chapel of the Magi which was begun by

Pietro da Como and rebuilt by Sammicheli. The choir has fine Gothic stalls and frescoes by Ugolino di Prete Illario who was assisted by Pinturicchio, and a large stained-glass window.

Next we find the right arm of the transept and the Cappella del Corporale where, behind the principal altar, is a canopy of marble mosaic containing a silver-gilt reliquary with the blood-stained chalice-cloth associated with the Miracle of Bolsena. The reliquary was executed by Ugolino di Maestro Vieri of Siena in 1337 and is one of the master-pieces of Italian goldsmiths' work.

Opposite the Cathedral is the Palazzo Faina, which has a priceless collection of Greek vases found in Etruscan tombs and, on the right, the Palazzo dei Papi or Palazzo Soliano whose name seems to be derived from an ancient Temple of the Sun which stood on its present site.

The large room on the first floor is the Art Gallery with fine sculptures by Nino and Giovanni Pisano, two projects for the Cathedral façade, an unfinished polyptych by Simone Martini, frescoes removed from two Etruscan tombs and several other interesting works of art.

Orvieto has many churches and palaces of less interest and I do not propose to list them. We should visit, however, Piazza del Popolo and its wonderful Palace of the same name built of beautiful golden-coloured tufa stone. This is an edifice of the mid-13th century in the Romano-Gothic style with massive arcades, a large flight of steps and attractive windows with three bays.

Taking Via della Pace with its ancient houses, we reach Piazza XXIX Marzo where the ancient Dominican convent, now used as barracks, has preserved an Etruscan oven. Alongside, the Church of S. Domenico of 1233 was the first in Italy to be dedicated to this saint. It has lost its nave and all that remains are the apse and transept with the tomb of Cardinal Guillaume de Braye by Arnolfo di Cambio and the underground Petrucci Chapel by Sammicheli.

From the funicular terminus we can descend as far as the ruins of the Augural Temple known as the Belvedere, an early 5th-century B.C. Etruscan temple, and see the well of the *Rocca* which was hewn by Clement VII in 1527 when he had sought refuge in Orvieto after the sack of Rome; fearing the town would be besieged and deprived of water, he wisely ordered a well to be dug. Il Pozzo di San Patrizio, so-named because it was similar to a cave of Saint Patrick in Ireland, was begun by Antonio da Sangallo the Younger in 1527 and finished by Mosca in 1540. It is partly hewn in the tufa, partly built of masonry, and is 200 feet deep and 42 feet wide. The bottom touches the tertiary marl below the tufa. Two separate spiral staircases wind round the shaft; water-carrying asses descended by one and ascended by the other.

An ogival gate leads to the ancient *Rocca* now used as a garden.

There now remain to be seen, below the plateau, the Etruscan necropolis and the Abbey of SS. Severo e Martirio.

The Necropolis of the Crucifix of Tufa, which dates from the 4th century B.C., consists of a series of single-chamber tombs made of squared blocks and arranged in regular rows. The name of the deceased can be read, engraved in stone, above the entrance.

Other tombs have been discovered on the other side of the valley near a Roman way which follows the arches of a 13th-century aqueduct. We can see several tombs, including that of the Lecate family, which was decorated with fine frescoes many of which have disappeared. Other tombs lie hidden beneath oak and chestnut trees awaiting discovery.

We leave by way of the Porta Romana and soon see rising before us, amidst cypress trees, the fine, 12-sided Romanesque campanile of the Abbey of SS. Severo e Martirio.

This Benedictine abbey was taken over in 1220 by Pre-monstratensians who enlarged the building by constructing a refectory, a cloister which has since been destroyed, and a chapter-house in the transitional Romano-Gothic style.

On arriving, we find, on the right, the Church of the Crucifix which is the ancient refectory with its large, slightly tierspoint nave. The apse has a wonderful 13th-century fresco portraying *The Crucifixion with Several Saints*.

Then, on the left, are the ivy-covered ruins of the chapter-house. We will enter a courtyard closed by the abbatial dwelling whose Roman-Gothic style is reminiscent of that of the Abbey of Casamari, with its massive arcades and attractive twin windows.

From the left, a wonderful semicircular arcade of 1221 leads to the ancient 12th-century church.

Taking the road we have recently left in order to reach the abbey, we will continue to Bagnoregio, enjoying fine views of Orvieto before it is finally out of sight.

Bagnoregio is the birthplace of Saint Bonaventura, the friend of Thomas Aquinas. There are several churches, the most interesting being that of S. Agostino which dates from the 11th century. In the 14th century it was transformed into the Gothic style and decorated with frescoes.

One kilometre away is La Civita perched on a tufa plateau. It has preserved a certain character with its entrance gate, its arcades and its portals covered with nettles.

We soon reach the N.71 which takes us to MONTEFIAS-CONE which is famous for its "Est, est, est" wines. The origin was a valet who preceded his master, a German prelate of the Fugger family of Augsburg, when travelling in order to test the wines at the various stopping places. On the doors of the hostelries where the best wine was to be had he inscribed the word "*est*" (Vinum *est* bonum), and when he reached the inn at Montefiascone ("bottle-mountain") he wrote the "*est*" three times on the door, with the result that his master never got any farther.

The most remarkable building in Montefiascone is the

ABBEY OF SS. SEVERO E MAR-
TIRIO, NEAR ORVIETO.

28. S. MARIA DELLA QUERCIA, N
VITERBO, CLOIST

. BAGNAIA, GARDENS OF VILLA
LENTE.

30. VITERBO, PALACE OF THE POP[

Church of S. Flaviano whose façade has a portico with three arcades surmounted by a balcony and a small loggia with slender Tuscan columns. The Romanesque part with Lombard arcades dates from the 12th century.

The interior consists of two superimposed buildings. The upper church, with three asymmetrical naves separated by low columns supporting semicircular or elliptical arcades, is really nothing more than large tribunes arranged over the side-aisles.

The lower church of 1032, remodelled in the early 14th century, also has three naves separated by pillars or columns of various forms with capitals which reveal an Etruscan influence on the sculptors of the 12th-century sculptors.

The most interesting part of the construction consists of three oven-shaped apses designed as a half circle and decorated with an attractive sculptured frieze.

The walls are for the most part still decorated with 14th-century frescoes. On entering we can see the tombstone of Johan Fugger with the inscription: EST, EST, EST. PR(*OPTER*) MIN(*IUM*) EST HIC IO(*ANNES*) DE FUGGER DO(*MINUS*) MEVS MORTVVS EST. ("Too much *Est, est, est* caused the death of my master, Johan Fugger.")

We can also see the Cathedral which was built in 1519 by Sammicheli. The interior is in the form of a hexagon and surmounted by an impressive cupola.

VITERBO, the next place on our route, is one of the most fascinating towns in Latium with its mediaeval quarter, its Bishop's Palace and its convents, some beyond the town. Viterbo has preserved most of its mediaeval walls which we skirt as we pass a gate, now walled-up, then the Porta della Verità with, opposite, the Church of S. Maria della Verità. It was founded in the 12th century by the Premonstratensians, enlarged and decorated in the 14th and 15th centuries, and is now the Civic Museum.

The Cappella Mazzatosta, one of its principal features, is decorated with frescoes by Lorenzo da Viterbo who completed the work in 1469. The simplicity of his style is admirable, notably in *The Marriage of the Virgin*. There are also other works of art, including paintings by Cavarozzi and Sebastiano del Piombo.

The cloister is in the Gothic style with groups of four tierspoint arcades separated by buttresses which support the columns of the upper gallery.

We will continue to skirt the mediaeval walls and facing the Porta Romana we will find an avenue leading to the Church of S. Maria in Gradi which was built in 1244, then rebuilt in a majestic style by Salvi in 1738.

The façade is fronted by an elegant portico of 1466. In the near-by convent which has been made into a penitentiary, we can see a fine Gothic cloister with tierspoint arcades in groups of five supported by coupled Romanesque slender columns of marble. It is difficult to obtain permission to see the second cloister which has an attractive octagonal fountain of 1480.

We enter Viterbo through the Porta Romana which was remodelled in 1653 in the Baroque style. On the right, we find the campanile of the Church of S. Sisto and the fine semicircular apse of the same 9th-century Romanesque church which was erected on the site of a pagan Temple and enlarged in the 12th century.

The interior is in the basilican plan, has three naves separated by six columns with convex shafts and interesting capitals. The altar dates from the 4th and 5th centuries and consists of architectronic fragments. Another pagan altar, which is decorated with bas-reliefs, was used for baptism by immersion. The raised choir is Romanesque with three naves separated by columns with interesting capitals and three apses added in the 12th century. The staircase is flanked by two Romanesque pulpits.

Piazza della Fontana Grande owes its name to a wonderful

fountain consisting of a basin in the form of a Greek cross, begun in 1206 by Bertoldo and Pietro di Giovanni.

We next reach Piazza del Comune, the centre of the town, which is decorated with two lions on granite columns. Opposite, the Palazzo Comunale, which was begun in 1460 and enlarged in the 16th century, has a picturesque court-yard with a portico and a loggia on the entrance side and, at the far end, a fine fountain by Caparozzi. Along the sides are six lids belonging to Etruscan sarcophagi. On the first floor are various rooms decorated with frescoes.

On this same *piazza* is the Palazzo del Capitano del Popolo which was greatly remodelled, also the Church of S. Angelo in Spata with, on the right of the portal, a Roman sarco-phagus decorated with bas-reliefs representing hunting scenes; it is known as The Tomb of the Beautiful Galiana. The latter was a woman of great beauty who lived in the first half of the 12th century and was called the sixth wonder of Viterbo. According to legend, a Roman baron whose advances she had spurned besieged the town and insisted Galiana appear on the ramparts; she did and he shot her dead with an arrow.

Let us take Via S. Lorenzo which passes the 15th-century Palazzo Chigi which is flanked by a mediaeval tower and has an attractive courtyard, then the Borgogone Tower and the Church of the Gesu which dates from the 11th century. Dante relates how on 13th March, 1272, Guy and Simon de Montfort stabbed Prince Henry of Cornwall, the son of Richard, Earl of Cornwall and King of the Romans, when he was attending Mass at this church, in revenge for the death of their father, Simon de Montfort, who had been executed by order of the royal family of England.

We will discover other towers and palaces before reaching the Cathedral Bridge which connects the town with the ancient castle. At the far end is the picturesque Palazzo Farnese, a fine early 15th-century edifice with elegant twin windows and a delightful courtyard. We next find another mediaeval house with remains of Etruscan walls, then finally reach Piazza del Duomo with, on the right, the Loggia and the Palace of the Popes which is fronted by a large flight of steps.

This is the most outstanding edifice of the mediaeval town. It was erected in 1257 when the popes often resided at Viterbo. The first storey has six large twin semicircular windows, and the elegant Gothic loggia is supported by a large arcade which itself is resting on a massive pillar.

A large room in the interior was used for the conclaves of 1271, 1276 and 1281 which respectively witnessed the election of Gregory X, John XXI and Martin V. It was during the election of the first named that Rainero Gatti, Captain of the People of Viterbo, on the advice of Saint Bonaventura, seeing that the cardinals could not reach an agreement, locked them in the palace, had the roof removed and reduced their supplies of food and drink. After 33 months of conclave Gregory X was finally elected.

The Cathedral at the far end of the *piazza* is a 12th-century Romanesque construction which was erected on the site of a Temple of Hercules and doubtless the work of Lombard architects who had settled at Viterbo in 1090. The façade was rebuilt in 1560. The interior has three naves which are separated by 20 beautiful monolithic columns with interesting capitals. The campanile was rebuilt during the second half of the 14th century.

We cross the bridge and reach the *piazza* where we find the Church of S. Maria Nuova which is of 1080 and one of the most interesting Romanesque works of Viterbo, surrounded by ancient houses. On an angle of its beautiful façade is a graceful pulpit from which Saint Thomas Aquinas preached.

After further walks through mysterious narrow streets and between mediaeval houses which we can take at our discretion, we leave Viterbo by the Porta Florentina or the Porta

Murata in order to take Via Trieste in the direction of Orte
but we first take notice, on the right, of the ancient convent
of S. Maria del Paradiso, now used as barracks, for its fine
13th-century Romano-Gothic cloister with trilobulate arcades. Three kilometres along the road we will stop in order
to see the most outstanding building in the surroundings of
Viterbo, the Church of S. Maria della Quercia, which is one
of the finest achievements of the Italian Renaissance. A flight
of steps leads to the austere embossed façade by Jacopo da
Firenzuola, with its three handsome portals and three rose-
windows, topped by a large triangular pediment with two
lions on each side of an oak tree. On the right, is the isolated
campanile with three richly decorated orders. The architect
was Ambrogio da Milano (1481).

In the interior, we can admire the three naves, a fine
ceiling, a wonderful tabernacle by Bregno, elegant stalls and
a harmonious two-storey cloister; the lower one is still
Gothic, and the upper is Renaissance. Of interest also is
another cloister in the Tuscan style and the refectory.

BAGNAIA is a picturesque town with its walls and towers
on the banks of a river. We reach a *piazza* which is not lacking in charm, with its fountain, a crenellated cylindrical tower
and the entrance gate of the castle, or the ancient town.

But what really interests us at Bagnaia are the gardens of
the Villa Lente, which we can visit on request. They were
designed by Vignola in 1564 for Cardinal Gambera, Bishop
of Viterbo, who wanted to make his villa a summer residence;
they were finished by his successor, Cardinal Montalto.
The villa then passed into the hands of the Lente family after
whom it is named.

An impressive wrought-iron grille leads to the formal
gardens which are designed around a monumental fountain
crowned by a statue of Pegasus by Giambologna. It is framed
by two small pavilions. Water from the wooded hill flowed
between them through the medium of fountains and a

cascade, designed as a long crayfish, finally reaches a canal which flows round a stone table where the cardinal placed his wine to cool and entertained his friends during summer evenings.

We will leave the road to Orte after ten kilometres in order to take that, on the left, to BOMARZO, a town of Etruscan origin where we find the Palazzo Orsini which was built in 1525 and finished by Vignola in 1565.

But we are interested above all in the fantastic garden which was created by Vicino Orsini shortly after 1561, at the foot of the hill. It long remained abandoned and unknown, but in recent years much has been written about the monsters of Bomarzo.

Unknown sculptors took advantage of the level rocks to create all kinds of fantastic monsters and animals such as elephants, urns, grottoes in the form of open jaws, a very lop-sided house, all mingled with garden elements then in vogue, fluted vases, balustrades, pine cones and nymphs with butterfly wings.

A graceful temple by Vignola with its Doric portico and cupola was probably the mausoleum of Giulia Farnese, the wife of Vicino Orsini.

We return to the main road, follow it for two kilometres and this time take the road on the right, the one to SORIANO NEL CIMINO where on a large rectangular *piazza* we find the 13th-century Collegiate Church with its neo-Classic interior and large baptismal fonts, also the crenellated castle which was enlarged in 1278 by Nicholas III who died there two years later. It is one of the finest in Latium, but it has now been made into a prison.

We can see also the Palazzo Chigi, an impressive work begun by Vignola, which consists of two main buildings supported by massive foundations. An embossed gate leads to a huge *piazza* which is decorated with statues. To the left we can see the Papacqua (Queen of the Water) Fountain hewn directly in the rock and a second group of buildings with a loggia opening on to a garden where other fountains of Venus, Pan and nymphs are likewise hewn in the rock.

The larger of the two palaces has a handsome vestibule with niches adorned with statues and on the first floor a room decorated by Vignola. The ceilings, the doors and the furniture date from the 18th century.

At VIGNANELLO we will find another impressive castle, that of Ruspoli, which is still surrounded by moats. This is a severe 16th-century construction with slightly projecting wings and entirely crowned by a watch-path on machicolation.

The town has preserved part of its walls and three gates.

A small road passes the delightful Madonna del Parto and leads to Fabrica di Roma, whose *Rocca*, with its high tower, still preserved, once belonged to the Farnese family.

We next pass through CARBOGNANO where we see the Baroque Church of S. Filippo, the baronial palace built by the Farnese which subsequently passed into the hands of the Sciarra, with its handsome square keep and attractive courtyard.

After leaving the town along the road to Caprarola, on the left, near the Church of S. Donato, we see the ruins, doubtless of a temple, dating from Republican times.

At CAPRAROLA we will discover one of the handsomest Renaissance palaces, the Palazzo Farnese, which was built by Alessandro Farnese, the grandson of Paul III. The foundations were by Peruzzi and Sangallo the Younger and it was about 1547 that Vignola undertook this very original work.

The building is on the summit of a hill overlooking the town and all the Cimini Mountains as far as Mont Soracte. The foundations are pentagonal in form, from which Vignola took great advantage.

As one comes from the town, one finds oneself facing a huge esplanade formed of various stepped terraces. Below the first is a portico with three embossed arcades topped by a balustrade. An easy slope leads to the first terrace where other ramps begin, framing the two embossed doors set into buildings which serve as the foundation for the second terrace on which the palace is built. These underground apartments could be reached by carriage.

In the centre of the palace is a magnificent circular court-yard enclosed by two storeys of porticos. The *salons* were decorated by the Zuccari brothers, Tempesta and Vignola.

The gardens surrounded by woods are among the finest secret gardens of the Italian Renaissance. The *palazzina*, built by Vignola and gracefully decorated, is fronted by a terrace with fountains, plots of box trees, stone seats and statues of canephores. Entrance is by means of two flights of steps bordered by walls and there is a chain of running water provided by a series of dolphins which spurt out the water running from the large river fountain. The whole is quite charming and it is now part of the summer residence of the President of the Republic.

RONCIGLIONE has preserved part of its mediaeval town. This lies beyond the castle of the Di Vico, which is flanked at each angle by a circular tower. There are several mediaeval and Renaissance houses, notably in Via Borgo di Sopro at Nos. 3–5 and 57. We leave, on the left, the ruined Church of S. Andrea with its fine campanile, and reach the Church of S. Maria della Providenza which also has a small Romanesque campanile.

Let us continue to SUTRI with its mingling of Etruscan and Roman remains and its mediaeval section, the houses closely set one against another built into the ancient Etruscan ramparts.

This important Etruscan centre was taken by the Romans in 391 B.C. and recaptured ten years later by the Etruscans. But that very day Furius Camillus again seized the town and his name is engraved on one of the five town gates, the Porta

Furia. The Etruscans besieged the town in vain in 310 and
311 B.C. Under Augustus it received a new colony of
inhabitants.

We will take Via Garibaldi and, passing the Palazzo
Comunale, we find the Cathedral which has been rebuilt but
preserved its Romanesque campanile and a crypt by
Lombard masters.

Next is the Bishop's Palace with its Gothic twin windows
and a fountain formed of an antique sarcophagus.

We leave the town by means of the Porta Vecchia where
we see Etruscan, Roman and mediaeval remains, then leave,
on the right, the Villa Savorelli where we find an Etruscan
tomb adapted to Christian use and fronted by a vestibule
with remains of frescoes. The church-tomb has three naves
separated by pillars, light is ensured by lateral windows, and
it is likewise decorated with frescoes.

In a handsome park surrounding the villa are the ruins of a
mediaeval castle known as that of Charlemagne, then farther
on, the amphitheatre, which is the principal archaeological
feature of Sutri.

It is entirely hewn in the tufa stone and was probably built
in the time of Augustus by Etruscan masters. It is elliptical,
almost circular, in shape and well preserved.

CAPRANICA is a colourful and picturesque town well
situated on its rock. The Romanesque Church of S. Francesco is interesting with, on the right, the Romanesque portal
of the hospital with its curious tympanum. There are also
several mediaeval and Renaissance houses.

We return to the Via Claudia which passes through Oriolo
Romano and Manziana before reaching BRACCIANO
which is dominated by the fine castle of the Orsini flanked,
on the town side, by three cylindrical towers and crowned by
crenels and machicolation.

Work was begun in 1470 by Napoleon Orsini, who used
the *Rocca* which already existed and finished by his son in

1485. In 1494 Charles VIII stayed here. In 1497 the castle was besieged in vain by Alexander VI. In 1696 Flavio Orsini sold it to the Odescalchi who in turn sold it in 1803 to the Torlonia, then repurchased it in 1848.

The castle is triangular in plan and its state of conservation makes it one of the most interesting in Latium. It can, moreover, be visited. There are ancient furnishings and several works of art. In the centre, the triangular courtyard has, on one side, a portico and a Romanesque loggia, and on the other, a Renaissance flight of steps, and on the third a fine Renaissance portal. Of interest also is the watch-path around the castle with fine views over Lake Bracciano.

We return to the Via Claudia which rejoins the previous itinerary near Veii.

ITINERARY VII

FROM FLORENCE TO ROME
BY WAY OF S. GIMIGNANO AND GROSSETO

Castelfiorentino — Certaldo — S. Gimignano —Volterra
— Pomarance — Massa Marittima — Grosseto.

WE leave Florence by the Porta Romana and, at Galluzzo, where we can visit the Certosa di Val d'Ema which I have described in the previous itinerary, we will take the road in the direction of Montespertoli and pass some 100 yards from the town of Giogoli where we will find an interesting 12th-century church.

We skirt, on the left, the park of the Villa dei Collazzi which was built in the 16th century from the design by Santi di Tito whose *Marriage of Cana* can be seen in the chapel.

We leave, on the right, at Tattoli, the fine 16th-century Villa dei Bini and pass through Cerbaia where on the *piazza* we find the Casa Bandinelli. A room on the ground floor is decorated with a fresco by Lorenzo di Bicci, representing *The Virgin and Child*, and *Saint Catharine and Other Saints*.

Farther on at Montegufoni are the remains of an ancient castle which belonged to the Acciaiuoli family, and, in our own times, to the Sitwell family. The church contains paintings by the School of Bernardo Daddi and Taddeo Gaddi.

We next reach Montespertoli, an ancient town whose 16th-century church has several interesting works of art. We can then continue as far as S. Pietro in Mercato whose

FLORENCE

Castelfiorentino
Certaldo
S.GIMIGNANO
Volterra

Pomarance

Massa Maritima

GROSSETO

FROM FLORENCE TO ROME
BY S. GIMIGNANO
AND GROSSETO

VITERBE
Tuscánia
S.Martino
al Cimino
Vetralla
Bieda

Talamone
Orbetello
Ansedonia
Tarquinia

Civitavecchia

Cerveteri

ROME

n

Ostia

fine Romanesque church also has several worthwhile works of art.

Next is CASTELFIORENTINO whose ancient part clings to a spur overlooking the Elsa.

From Piazza Antonio Gramsci we can see the Church of S. Francesco which was begun in 1213 with its high brick façade decorated with coats-of-arms and its single-nave interior with timbered roof. The 15th-century frescoes which once decorated the walls have been removed to Florence.

Behind, in a large meadow, is the Church of S. Verdiana which was rebuilt in the early 18th century with a Baroque façade having two orders, fronted by a portico. The architect was Bernardo Fallani. A small art gallery has several interesting pictures.

We next find the Church of S. Chiara which has several 15th-century paintings and we should not fail to visit the 15th-century Church of the Visitation which is entirely decorated with frescoes by Benozzo Gozzoli and his pupils.

We will now take the road which ascends the broad fertile valley of the Elsa and soon reach CERTALDO which is the birthplace of Boccaccio to whom naturally the principal *piazza* is dedicated, together with its statue. Boccaccio's house was destroyed during aerial bombardment in the last war, but has been rebuilt. The poet's cenotaph can be seen in the 13th-century Church of SS. Michele e Jacopo. The interior has a single nave with timbered ceiling and semicircular apse.

The most interesting building in Certaldo is the Palazzo Pretorio which at the close of the 13th century belonged to Count Alberti, then to Florentine priests and chieftains. It was entirely rebuilt in the 15th century. This is a handsome building with two rows of windows and crowned with crenels with, on the façade, the enamelled terracotta coat-of-arms of the priests. The ancient loggia, on the left, is decorated with coats-of-arms and frescoes.

In the interior, we can see several interesting rooms, including one with frescoes by Pier Francesco Fiorentino. The courtyard is picturesque with its portico, its loggia and its flight of steps.

Of interest also, in the near-by Via Rivellino, is the ancient Church of S. Tommaso with its Romano-Gothic façade and, at No. 3, the remains of a fine Romanesque cloister opposite a massive tower.

We leave the valley of the Elsa for the road to S. Gimignano which crosses hills planted with olive groves, but six kilometres before arriving there, we reach an intersection and, taking the road on the left, we will continue to CELLOLE where, at the far end of the village, in a *piazza* shaded by cypress trees, we find the Pieve di Cellole, a Romanesque parish church which was built of travertine and finished in 1238. The pure façade has a handsome portal, two simple bays and a twin one above.

The interior has three naves, which are separated by cylindrical pillars with crude capitals, and a timbered ceiling. The semicircular apse is decorated with rich blind arcades resting on slender columns. The window is framed by piers with luxurious arabesques.

There are octagonal baptismal fonts hewn from a single block of stone. A door, on the right, leads to a garden with a fine view of the exterior of the apse which likewise is decorated with blind arcades.

Two kilometres farther on we pass the Oratory of S. Bilgio which dates from the 13th or 14th century. Then, standing on its hill, we soon discover the proud-looking town of S. GIMIGNANO bristling with towers.

We enter by the Porta S. Matteo of 1262 which is built in the Sienese style. From here we have a fine view over the surrounding countryside with its rolling pattern of hills planted with vineyards and olive groves and dotted with cypress trees.

Now that our large cities are overwhelmed by the trap-
pings of modern life, we must turn to such decaying,
forgotten towns as San Gimignano in their purely
country setting in order to find intact any reminiscence of
the past. And there is none that recalls the proud,
noisy life of the free towns of mediaeval Italy better than San
Gimignano. Its *piazze* and streets with their fortified houses
and high towers are almost as they were in the days when
the Ardenghelli and the Salvucci, the Guelfs and the
Ghibellines, the partisans of Siena and of Florence defied
each other until the time when the latter imposed their
domination in 1353.

Built in the 12th, 13th and 14th centuries, these towers
earned for San Gimignano the name, "The City of Beautiful
Towers." 72 of these existed in 1580, but only 15 are still
standing.

Since we have entered the town by the Porta S. Matteo,
let us first see, on a near by isolated *piazza*, with its well in
the centre, the Romano-Gothic Church of S. Agostino whose
pure façade is flanked by a slender steeple and has four
Gothic windows on the side.

The huge single-nave interior has timbered vaulting and
terminates in three tierspoint apses. On the right, the Chapel
of S. Bartolo has a wrought-iron grille and, behind, a
wonderful marble altar by Benedetto da Maiano and
frescoes by Sebastian Mainardi.

In the right apse there is a *Nativity of the Virgin* of 1523 by
Vincenzo Tamagni and frescoes by Bartolo di Fredi, but we
must admire, above all, in the choir, a *Coronation of the Virgin
and Several Saints* by Piero del Pollaiolo of 1483 and splendid
frescoes by Benozzo Gozzoli and his pupils, notably by
Giusto d'Andrea. Together with the *Magi* in the Palazzo
Riccardi in Florence, these frescoes are some of the most
expressive the artist ever did and have much grace, vitality
and picturesqueness. He portrays *The Life of Saint Augustine*

in 17 frescoes on three rows, ending with several scenes
devoted to other subjects.

In the left nave we find a fresco by Sebastiano Mainardi
portraying *Saint Gimignano and Several Famous Inhabitants of the
City*, then, on the third altar, a fine *Saint Sebastian Protecting
Men from the Anger of God* by Gozzoli. *The Descent from the
Cross* on the first altar is by Tamagni.

From the sacristy we enter the 15th-century cloister with
an arcaded gallery supported by elegant slender columns
surmounted by a loggia with fine Gothic windows. The
chapter-house opens on to the cloister by two beautiful
Gothic windows.

On the right, the small Church of S. Pietro is an 11th-
century Romanesque structure with a simple façade and a
rose-window. The left side has Pre-Romanesque windows
and a campanile.

The interior has a single nave and timbered roof. The walls
are decorated with 11th-century frescoes by the Sienese
School and the painting on the high altar is attributed to
Giovanni Cambi (1531).

We reach Via Folgore da S. Gimignano where, at No. 19,
we find the Conservatory of Saint Clara where the small
Church of S. Chiara has, on the high altar, a painting by
Matteo Rosselli and on the left altar, another by Vincenzo
Tamagni. From the terrace of the Institute there is a fine
view of the towers of San Gimignano, which we must not
neglect to see.

Somewhat farther on, we find the long façade of the
Hospital of S. Fina of 1203 with its ancient chapel which was
made into a vestibule in the 15th century and decorated with
busts by Torrigiani and frescoes by Mainardi, and then the
unfinished façade of the Church of S. Girolamo with its late
15th-century frescoes and others by Tamagni. In the
refectory of the near-by monastery is a large fresco by two
pupils of Ghirlandaio.

I. MONSTERS OF BOMARZO.

32. CAPRAROLA, PALAZZO FARNES

Close to the wall is the Romanesque Church of S. Jacopo which was built in the 13th century by the Templars. The façade, whose lower part is of brick and upper of stone, has a Pisan portal surmounted by a beautiful rose-window and the cornice is decorated with majolica bowls.

The interior has a single Gothic nave with pillars set against the wall, tierspoint arcades and ogival vaulting. The pillars are decorated with several paintings, notably a *Crucifixion* which is attributed to Memmo di Filippuccio, the father of Lippo Memmi.

Taking the arcade to the right of the church from which there is a fine view over the other side of the town, we will follow the road which runs along the wall built in 1262 and reach the beautiful Porta delle Fonti. Beyond are the Fonti, a series of ten arcades, some semicircular, others tierspoint, which date from the 12th and 14th centuries and within which are basins for washing wool.

Let us continue to follow the outer walls to the Porta S. Giovanni, which is the gate by which one usually arrives from Florence by way of Poggibonsi or Siena.

From here there is a fine panoramic view of the country-side and town with the massive, cylindrical Bastion of S. Francesco. The gate itself, with its crenels and machicolation, built in 1262, is the finest one in San Gimignano. In 1691 the lovely Baroque Church of la Madonna dei Lumi was added to it.

We will follow Via Giovanni, which is directly in front of us, between high 12th-century houses. At No. 99, is a tabernacle with a fresco by Mainardi, then the remains of the Pisan-Romanesque 13th-century façade of S. Francesco; at No. 61, a late 13th-century house-tower; at No. 40, the remains of the Convent of S. Caterina of 1353; at No. 44, the 14th-century Palazzo Pratellesi with its tower; and finally, fronted by the Arco dei Becci, the Palazzo Cugnanesi with its very high tower.

We now reach the heart of the town at Piazza Cisterna, which is in the form of a triangle and entirely bordered by ancient houses and palaces. After seeing so many historical settings spoilt by bad taste, it is a delight to discover one which has escaped degradation, with its well in the centre and its brick paving arranged in a fishbone design. At No. 22 is the finest palace of all, the Palazzo Friani, with its two rows of lovely twin windows which are typical of 14th-century Siena and its massive Torre del Capitano del Popolo.

The adjacent Piazza del Duomo is also paved with brick and has the same design. Framed by high towers, it is especially impressive as it contains the most important buildings of San Gimignano: the Collegiate Church, the Palazzo del Popolo and the Palazzo del Podestà.

The latter, rebuilt in 1239 and enlarged in 1337, is flanked by the high Rognosa Tower. Partly of brick and partly of stone, the façade had a large arcade which leads to the interior.

The Palazzo del Popolo, which was begun in 1288 and enlarged in 1323, has a façade crowned with Guelf crenels, is decorated with coats-of-arms and flanked by the Torre Grossa (Heavy Tower) begun in 1300. It was said that each new *podestà* endeavoured to increase its height.

We will enter a picturesque courtyard and, taking a flight of steps heading to a loggia, we reach the impressive Sala di Dante, so called because it was here on 8th May, 1300, that Dante addressed the *podestà* and the council about the necessity of a Guelf league in Tuscany. On the right wall is a fine *Virgin Enthroned with Saints* by Lippo Memmi which is as fine a work as that painted by Simone Martini in the Palazzo Pubblico in Siena. Other late 13th-century frescoes are reminiscent of Duccio's style and represent different scenes, including hunting, castle life and festivities. There are beautiful ceramic pieces in other rooms. The second floor is now a museum and has two first-class works of art, an *Annunci-*

ation by Filippino Lippi and a very colourful *Virgin and Child with Several Saints* by Pinturicchio, as well as other paintings dealing with the town of San Gimignano. Fascinating frescoes portray daily life in the 14th century. We can climb up to the top of the tower, which is the tallest one in the town, to enjoy the fine view of the lovely countryside.

On our way down, we should ask to see, beneath the loggia, two frescoes by Il Sodoma and another attributed to Taddeo di Bartolo.

The Collegiate Church, which is also known as the Cathedral and reached by means of a large flight of steps, is a Romanesque edifice that was consecrated in 1148 and transformed in 1456 by Giuliano da Majano.

The interior has three naves separated by columns. The transept crossing and the choir were enlarged by Giuliano da Majano who built the Chapel of S. Fina, that of la Conception and the new sacristy. The walls are decorated with frescoes which were damaged by aerial bombardment, but which have been restored.

As San Gimignano lay between Florence and Siene, artists of both cities were in turn summoned to work here. The Sienese painted the lateral walls and most of the reverse side of the façade and therefore occupy most of the wall surface. They all belong to the second half of the 13th century. On the reverse side of the façade Taddeo di Bartolo painted a fanciful *Last Judgment* with *Paradise* on the left and *Hell* on the right which is next to a *Martyrdom of Saint Sebastian* by the Florentine Benozzo Gozzoli and a fine polychrome-wood *Annunciation* by Jacopo della Quercia.

In the right nave we can see a series of frescoes devoted to the New Testament by a painter named Barna da Siena. Vasari tells how he died in 1381 after falling from the scaffolding while painting the *Crucifixion*. The work was continued by his nephew and pupil, Giovanni d'Ascio.

The frescoes are arranged in three rows. The most moving

scenes are *The Annunciation, The Baptism of Christ, The Call of Saint Peter, The Marriage of Cana, The Treachery of Judas* and *Christ on the Mount of Olives.*

The frescoes in the left nave devoted to the Old Testament are by the Sienese Bartolo di Fredi. We can criticise the drawing, colour and composition, but they undeniably have a certain freshness and exuberance.

If we return to the right nave, we will find, at the far end, the Chapel of S. Fina which is a Renaissance jewel, the work, as I said, of Giuliano and Benedetto da Majano. Above the arcades is a polychrome terracotta frieze of seraphim. The marble altar is a sumptuous work by Benedetto da Majano whose work can be seen at Santa Croce and in the Palazzo Strozzi, in Florence. But it is above all the frescoes by Ghirlandaio which attract our attention, notably the scene portraying *Saint Gregory Announcing to Saint Fina Her Approaching Death.* Full of grace and simplicity, this may well be the artist's masterpiece. *The Saint's Funeral* and *The Angels Bearing Her off to Heaven* are also by the same artist, but the other frescoes are the work of his pupils, notably Mainardi, who painted the prophets and the saints in the spandrels.

The transept crossing was decorated by Giovanni Cambi and the choir panelling by Antonio da Colle, while the central nave has busts of the Apostles by Peir. Francesco Fiorentino, the first vault is probably by Ghirlandaio and the *Pietà* of the triumphal arch by Mainardi.

If we enter the Oratory of S. Giovanni, we will see an *Annunciation* by Ghirlandaio and baptismal fonts by Giovanni di Cecco.

From the Collegiate Church, by way of the Arco di S. Giovanni, we reach an isolated *piazza* which is bordered by the austere 12th–13th-century Palazzo della Prepositura which contains a museum devoted to sacred art with works from various churches.

We next pass behind the apse of the Collegiate Church in

order to see the ruins of the *Rocca* which was built by the Florentines in 1353 and dismantled in 1555 by order of Cosimo I. Octagonal in plan, it had two curtain walls and a tower at each angle. From here there are fine views over the town and its towers.

Let us return to Piazza del Duomo and take Via S. Matteo, the most picturesque street in the town, bordered, especially on the right, by mediaeval buildings.

Of interest are, on the left, the Salvucci Towers; at No. 16, the Pettini Palace and Tower; the Arch and Palace of the Chancellery dating from the close of the 13th century; the 13th-century Church of S. Bartolo with, opposite, the Casa Bagnolesi; then at No. 27, the 14th-century Palazzo Mari.

On the left, we see successively at No. 32, the Pesciolini house-tower, which is a typical example of a fine 13th-century Florentine building; others at Nos. 36, 38, 44, 45, 52 and 58; then, at No. 60–62, the Palazzo Tinacci, which is one of the most outstanding palaces in San Gimignano; at No. 95 the equally handsome Palazzo Vichi and at No. 6 the Palazzo Mainardi.

We can now leave the town by way of Porta S. Matteo and travel outside the walls as far as Porta S. Giovanni from where we can visit the Monastery of Monte Oliveto, which we must not confuse with the famous convent of the same name. Taking a small road, on the right, we reach it within less than two kilometres.

The monastery was founded in 1340 and enlarged in 1458. The church with its stone façade fronted by a portico is flanked by a fine brick campanile. The interior is Baroque and the sacristy Renaissance. A handsome 15th-century cloister is enclosed on three sides by porticos. A *Crucifixion* was painted by a pupil of Benozzo Gozzoli from a drawing by the master.

By way of S. Donato, where we can see a beautiful 11th–12th-century Pisan church, we return to the N.68 at Castel

S. Gimignano, an important 14th-century fortress which is fairly well preserved, leaving on the left, on a height, the ruins of Torre di Montemiccioli, we cross a countryside of gentle hills to reach VOLTERRA, an ancient Etruscan town which was built like an acropolis overlooking the valleys of the Era and the Cécina.

The ancient *Velathri* overlooks a series of volcanic cones whose craters are extinct although underground fires are still smouldering. Here and there solfatras emerge with hot springs gushing forth and columns of vapour rising from the ground. Slabs of white clay manifest themselves in the midst of fields, and the flanks of the rocky plateau which supports "the silent town", as d'Annunzio called it, are still shaken by the baneful forces which cause fissures to appear, which often allow torrents of mud to escape.

One night about 200 years ago a huge section of rock broke away, weakened by the inner fire, and crashed at the far end of the valley, freeing torrents of mud and engulfing a mediaeval abbey built on the edge of the plateau. It carried off all the funeral furnishings of an Etruscan necropolis as well.

This deep ravine still exists and is called *Le Balze*, which we will see during the course of our visit.

The tourist wrongly neglects Volterra which, in addition to its Etruscan ruins, has preserved its mediaeval appearance with its severe palaces and its winding streets.

Volterra was one of the most powerful of the Etruscan towns. It founded Arezzo and Fiesole and defended the country from Ligurian pillagers. It became Roman in the 3rd century B.C. and withstood a siege by Sulla's troops for two years. It afterwards became a Roman *municipium*. In the 12th century it became a free town and overthrew its bishop and lords; then, with San Gimignano, it sided with the Guelfs; it accepted the suzerainty of Octaviano Belforti in the 14th century, but ordered his son to be decapitated; then, at last, it fell under the domination of Florence.

The Etruscan wall was much more extensive than the mediaeval one (about four and a half miles in circumference instead of two). It is well-preserved and we can follow it almost completely.

The road which leads to the town winds around the sides of the hill, then reaches Piazza dei Priori which is one of the most characteristic mediaeval *piazze* in Italy. It is more monumental than the one we have just seen at San Gimignano, but also more affected by modern life. It is bordered by the right side of the Cathedral and an entire series of palaces: the Bishop's Palace, the Palazzo Pretorio and above all the Palazzo dei Priori, with its austere façade. This palace was begun in 1208; it has twin ogival windows and is surmounted by crenels. It is flanked, on the right, by a high pentagonal tower and the vestibule which has ogival vaulting is decorated with many coats-of-arms. We can visit the Council Room and the Art Gallery with its interesting collection, including works by Rosso Fiorentino, Luca Signorelli, Taddeo di Bartolo, Stefano d'Antonio Vanni, Taddeo di Bartolo, Ghirlandaio, Riccio, and Daniele da Volterra.

We will skirt the Romanesque side of the Cathedral in order to see, on the near-by *piazza*, the façade of this Romanesque edifice which was erected in the 12th century but remodelled in the second half of the 13th in the Pisan style. Shouldered by buttresses and its gable decorated with blind arcades, the façade has a handsome marble portal. The tympanum is decorated with geometrical mosaics, and a rose-window.

The interior, which was remodelled in the 16th century, has three naves separated by columns coated with stucco whose capitals of 1584 are by Ricciarelli. The central nave has a fine coffer-ceiling with busts of Saints by Capriani executed by Pavolino.

On the reverse side of the façade is a handsome Romanesque forealtar, then in the transept there is a wonderful

Descent from the Cross, a polychrome-wood sculpture by a Pisan artist of the mid-13th century. In the first chapel we find the *Arca de S. Ottaviano* by Raphael Cioli of 1522 and in the choir a monumental marble ciborium, two angels by Mino da Fiesole, splendid Gothic stalls and the episcopal pulpit of 1404.

The pulpit, which was partly rebuilt in the 17th century with 12th-century elements, is by sculptors who were pupils of Guglielmo Pisano. Four slender columns, which are resting on two lions, an ox and a bull with satanic features, support the pulpit whose bas-reliefs represent *The Sacrifice of Abraham*, *The Last Supper*, *The Annunciation* and *The Visitation*.

Opposite the Cathedral is the isolated 13th-century baptistery which is octagonal in plan. The side facing the Cathedral is faced with white and green marble and has a Romanesque portal with the heads of *Jesus*, *Mary* and *The Apostles* on the architrave, and a twin window.

In the simple, bare interior, we can see a holy-water basin which consists of an Etruscan *cippus*, an altar with an elegant decoration by Mino da Fiesole and fine baptismal fonts by Andrea Sansovino.

The Diocesan Museum, which is reached by means of the portico of the Bishop's Palace, contains interesting works of art, notably a terracotta bust by Andrea della Robbia, reliquary busts and a gilt-bronze *Christ on the Cross* by Giambologna.

We then reach Via Ricciarelli, which has preserved its mediaeval appearance with the Buonparenti house-tower and other houses and palaces all dating from the 13th century. At No. 12, we find the Palazzo Ricciarelli with its rustic-embossed façade. This palace was once inhabited by Daniele da Volterra.

Via Buonparenti is also bordered by ancient houses: at No. 3, the 15th-century Casa Miranceli with elegant terracotta Gothic arcades on the second storey; at No. 7, the

15th-century Palazzo Bartolini. We reach Piazza Minucci where the palace of the same name, attributed to Antonio da Sangallo the Elder, has an elegant inner courtyard with arcades, although these are in bad condition. We leave, on the left, a mediaeval house at No. 2 Via Mandorlo and continue along Via dei Sarti with, at Nos. 17–19, the 15th-century Palazzo Viti whose fine Renaissance façade is attributed to Bartolommeo Ammanati. We reach the Church of S. Michele Arcangelo with its fine Pisan-Romanesque façade flanked below by columns. On the tympanum of the high portal is a marble *Virgin and Child* by the 14th-century Pisan School.

The *piazza* is dominated by the Toscano House-Tower which consists of an embossed 13th-century tower and a 14th-century house. In 1814 a theatre was built in the courtyard.

Taking Via di Dicciola with its picturesque flights of steps bordered by cypress trees, we reach the beautiful Fontana di Dicciola which was built in 1245 from the design of a master named Stefano and consists of two large ogival arcades containing a rectangular basin. Opposite, the Porta di Dicciola is of the 13th century.

We reach Piazza XX Settembre where we find the 15th-century Oratory of S. Antonio Abate and the 13th-century Church of S. Agostino which was rebuilt in 1728 and has three naves.

Somewhat farther on is the Guarnacci Museum which contains one of the most interesting Etruscan collections in Italy. Those of us who have chosen this itinerary in order to travel from Florence to Rome by way of Volterra, Tarquinia and Cerveteri can introduce ourselves to the Etruscan civilisation where originality is just beginning to be known.

At Volterra, we will find more than 600 funerary urns, almost all dating from the Hellenistic period (4th–1st centuries B.C.), the most ancient necropoli having for the

most part been engulfed by the lava of *Le Balze* which we
will shortly see. Many of these urns, which are adorned
with bas-reliefs, show a strong Greek influence, notably the
vases.

We pass the Church of S. Pietro in Selci with its Baroque
façade and the Conservatorio Feminile di S. Pietro which
contains interesting works of art, notably a fine polychrome
Annunciation which is attributed to Francesco di Valdambrino.

We next reach the *Rocca*, which is one of the most impressive
in all Italy, built entirely of brick on the foundations of the
ancient Etruscan acropolis. On the east, the Rocca Vecchia
(Old Castle) which is trapezoidal in plan, was built in 1343
by Walter de Brienne, Duke of Athens, then modified by
Lorenzo the Magnificent with a semielliptical tower known
as La Femmina. On the west, the Rocca Nuova, square in
place, is flanked by five towers, one of which, the keep, was
erected by Lorenzo the Magnificent after 1472. Since 1818
the fortress has been used as a prison and can be visited only
by authorisation of the Minister of Justice.

We will retrace our steps and find other mediaeval houses
in Via Matteoti: at No. 11, the Renaissance Palazzo Maffei;
then, at No. 7 Vicolo delle Prigioni, the 14th-century Palazzo
Rossi.

We will continue by way of the Porta all'Arco which has
preserved the outlines of the Etruscan path and is characterised by the shops of artisans in alabaster who seem to have
inherited the skill of the original Etruscan workers. This takes
us to the Arco Etrusco, one of the ten gates which gave access
to the interior of the town and the only one remaining,
together with the Porta Diana, which is nothing more than a
simple opening flanked by pillars composed of massive
blocks. The Porta all'Arco is not only the most ancient
Etruscan gate to have survived, but it has also preserved its
original design. Formed of blocks of tufa stone 40 inches long

and carefully squared, the arch was framed by two towers
during the Tyrrhenian period. During the Middle Ages
walls of quadrangular stones were added to it, but the vaulting
and arches of yellowish white travertine above the two sides
are still Etruscan. On the outer side, the three massive
projecting heads sculptured in black tufa stone, were doubtless those of gods—perhaps Jupiter and the Dioscuri—who
guarded the town.

There now remains for us to see the most unusual part of
Volterra, which we can visit either on foot or, better still, by
car. In this case we skirt the outer walls of the town until we
reach the Porta S. Felice with, alongside, the Fonte S. Felice
with its large ogival arcades.

Making a detour, we can descend as far as Borgo S.
Alessandro with the small Church of S. Alessandro and its
handsome Romanesque portal.

From the Porta S. Felice we reach the Church of S. Lino
of 1480 which according to tradition was erected on the site
of the house of Saint Lino, the second Pope. A Renaissance
portal leads to a nave whose vaulting is decorated with
frescoes.

Shortly afterwards, we find the 13th-century Church of
S. Francesco. Although greatly remodelled, it will interest us,
above all, for the Chapel of la Croce di Giorno built in 1315
with its own access to the *piazza*, on the right of the church
façade. The chapel consists of two Gothic bays which terminate in an apse and it is entirely decorated with frescoes.
The Evangelists on the vaulting of the first bay are by Jacopo
da Firenze and all the others by Cenni di Francesco Cenni.
The subject is the Legend of the Holy Cross. The frescoes
were inspired by those painted by Agnolo Gaddi in the
Church of S. Croce in Florence.

Opposite, the Church of S. Dalmazio has a Renaissance
portal. The Porta S. Francesco is the most impressive gate in
the entire town.

We pass beneath it and follow Via del Borgo di S. Stefano
with, on the right, the remains of the Pisan-Romanesque
Church of S. Stefano. Then making a turning to the left, we
soon seen the remains of the Etruscan wall of S. Chiara.

The fortifications of *Velathri* are among the most ancient
and gigantic in all Etruria. Begun in certain sections in the
second half of the 6th century B.C. and finished a century
later, they are 45 feet high.

We see the ancient Convent of S. Chiara with its church
fronted by a portico attributed to Ammanati, then take
Via Borgo S. Giusto which passes near four isolated columns
in a meadow surrounded by cypress trees, supporting terracotta statues of the town's patron saints. We reach the flight
of steps which leads to the Church of SS. Gusto e Clemente
which was begun in 1628 and contains a fine fresco by
Volterrano, *Elijah Sleeping.*

We reach the edge of *Le Balze,* that impressive ravine
which I have mentioned and which engulfed not only the
most ancient Etruscan necropolis but also the Church of
S. Clemente, the original Church of S. Giusto, the Monastery
of S. Marco and the most outlying houses of the town.

We can also see the Church of La Badia with its Baroque
façade which was rebuilt after the earthquake of 1846 with
its 16th-century cloister by Ammanati and its refectory
decorated with frescoes by Donato Muscagni.

Of interest also at Vallebuona are the recently discovered
remains of the Roman theatre dating from the Imperial
period.

We will take the road in the direction of Massa Marittima
which passes through Saline where salt mines already existed
in the 9th century. Then after having skirted the Cécina,
which we cross by a bridge which gives us a lovely view over
the surrounding countryside with its olive groves, we reach
Pomarance built on a height where the bishops of Volterra
had a castle. The church has a Romanesque façade and an

Annunciation by Il Pomarancio, who was born in the town; in the same street there are several ancient houses.

The road bends, winds among hills and passes in front of the Rocca di Silano and, more to the right, that of Monte-castelli which is enclosed by ruined walls; it winds around Monte S. Michele leaving, on the right, the baths of the same name, passes through Montecerboli and reaches Larderello in the centre of a region rich in hot water springs which have given birth to a borax industry.

The road next mounts towards Castelnuovo di Val di Cécina, a large town in the centre of steam volcanoes, then continues between slopes covered with oak and chestnut trees following the Pavone River through an Alpine land-scape. It rises and crosses an almost desert-like region, descends to Bivio and soon reaches MASSA MARITTIMA.

This town, which has an excellent situation on a hill surrounded by several torrents, was an episcopal seat as early as the 9th century. It was destroyed by the Saracens in 935, but flourished in the Middle Ages, thanks to its copper and silver mines. The Città Vecchia or Lower Town is essentially Romanesque, while the Città Nuova is Gothic. The ancient part is enclosed by walls with numerous gates decorated with coats-of-arms. The original *enceinte*, which was partly torn down in 1377, was rebuilt according to the present plan.

We reach Piazza Garibaldi where we find the most interesting monuments, notably the Cathedral. Built entirely of a warm golden-coloured stone, it was begun in the early 13th century in the Pisan-Romanesque style. The choir and apse were enlarged in 1287 in the Gothic style by an architect who also was Pisan.

The elegant façade is divided into two rows. The lower one is decorated with seven blind arcades. To heighten the perspective effect, those on the left are narrower. The architrave of the portal is decorated with scenes depicting

The Life of Saint Cerbone. The archivolts are richly sculptured
and the capitals topped by figures of lions. The lower row
consists of two superimposed loggias with blind arcades.
The far wall with its white and red bands has a large rose-
window. The lateral façades are also decorated with blind
arcades and have two portals. The wall of the central nave
has white and green bands and an attractive decoration of
blind arcades. At the far end rises the massive campanile.

The interior has three naves separated by columns of
unequal height with Corinthian or composite capitals which
are delicately sculptured and decorated with foliage or
animals. At the entrance to the right nave is the baptistery
which has wonderful reliefs by Giroldo da Como (1267) and
is surmounted by a 15th-century tabernacle.

The apse has fine 15th-century stalls; and the Chapel of
the Virgin a beautifully designed *Madonna delle Grazie* by the
Sienese School, 1316 being a likely date.

A staircase leads to the underground church consisting of
the Chapel of the Relics, which contains interesting examples
of goldsmiths' work, and of the lower polygonal-shaped apse
where we can see the Tomb of Saint Cebone, a charming
14th-century masterpiece by Goro di Gregorio, decorated
with eight bas-reliefs devoted to the Saint's life.

On leaving the Cathedral, we find the Bishop's Palace
which has been entirely rebuilt, then the Palazzo dell'-
Abbondanza with its three massive ogival arcades, built on
the ancient public fountain and once used as a store loft,
and on Piazza Garibaldi the Palazzo Pretorio, the ancient
residence of the *podestà*. This severe edifice entirely composed
of travertine was built in 1230. It consists of a ground floor
fronted by a double flight of steps and two rows of twin
windows which were topped by Ghibelline crenels.

The road to Follónica makes a rapid descent among olive
groves and has fine views over Maremma. We join the N.1
which, at first straight, leaving on the right Gavorrano on its

hill, then winds towards the south. On the left we see the tower of VETULONIA which is but five kilometres from the road. If we wish, we can visit Vetulonia, the ancient name (used again since 1887) of the village of Colonna.

It was one of the 12 Etruscan *lucumones* and it is from here that the Romans took their magisterial insignia: the fasces of the lictors, the curule chair, the purple toga and the brazen trumpets.

At the upper part of the town are the remains of the walls, consisting of huge parallelepipeds finished by smaller size stones. Below lies the necropolis with its ancient mound tomb which date from the 7th century B.C. From the 5th century onwards the most conspicuous tombs were desecrated and plundered. The objects which were discovered in the tombs left intact have been moved to the Archaeological Museum in Florence.

We leave Giuncarico on the left, and coming out on to the Grosseto Plain, we cross it in a straight line.

GROSSETO consists of a New and an Old Town surrounded by bastion walls in a hexagonal plan. This *enceinte*, which is reminiscent of that of Lucca, was begun in 1574 by Francesco I from the designs of Baldassare Lanci, who made use of the 14th-century Sienese walls, and it was finished in 1590 by Ferdinando I.

In the Old Town we find the Cathedral which was rebuilt in 1294 by Sozzo di Pace Rustichini by the enlargement of a more ancient church. The façade was rebuilt in the 19th century and several elements, such as capitals, were kept. The portal on the right side is by Sozzo. The 15th-century campanile on the left side was remodelled.

The interior consists of three naves separated by pillars and was subsequently dressed up in the Baroque taste. However, we can admire a fine *Assumption* by Matteo di Giovanni and baptismal fonts by Antonio di Ghino (1470).

The Museum of Sacred Art contains interesting works of

art, including a *Last Judgment* by the Workshop of Guido da Siena and a beautiful *Virgin with Child* by Sassetta.

We can see also the 13th-century Church of S. Francesco with its Gothic façade and single-nave interior with timbered vaulting. It contains interesting works of art. Alongside, there are the remains of a cloister with a Renaissance well.

We return to the Via Aurelia and follow the coastal route to Rome, which I shall be covering in a further Itinerary.

GLOSSARY

ABACUS: Flat slab on top of a capital.

ABUTMENT: Solid masonry placed to resist the lateral pressure of a vault.

ACANTHUS: Plant with thick fleshy and scalloped leaves copied as part of decoration of a Corinthian capital and in some types of leaf-carving.

ACROTERION: Pedestal for a statue at the angle of the pediment.

AEDICULE: Small structure sheltering altar or image of household god; small pedimented structure over a niche.

AMBULACRUM: Covered way.

AMBULATORY: Open or covered arcade or cloister; an aisle around a choir.

ANTA: Pilaster terminating the side wall of a Greek temple with the base and capital differing from those of adjacent columns.

ANTIPHONARY: Book of chants or anthems.

APSE: Eastern end of church containing Bishop's Throne.

APSIDIOLE: Secondary apse.

ARCADE: Range of arches supported on piers or columns, free-standing. BLIND ARCADE: Arcade set against a wall.

ARCHITRAVE: Lowest division of entablature resting on capitals of supporting column. Collective name for various parts surrounding a door or window.

ARCHIVOLT: Moulding curving round the under surface of an arch.

ARKOSE: Rock composed of quartz and felspar.

ARMARIUM: Cupboard or chest.

ASTRAGAL: Small moulding round top or bottom of column.

ATRIUM: Open central court in Greek and Roman churches: forecourt in early Christian churches.

BALDACHIN: Canopy, supported on pillars or fastened to wall, over throne, pulpit, altar, etc.

BARBICAN: Outwork defending the entrance to a castle.

BAROQUE: Style with sinuous lines, scrolls and exuberant carved ornaments, named after the painter Federigo Barocci, from Urbino (1528–1612). Born in Rome as a reaction against severe classical Renaissance, it spread throughout Europe.

BARTIZAN: Turret projecting from mediaeval tower.

BASILICA: In mediaeval architecture an aisled church with a clerestory.

BAS-RELIEF: Figures not standing far out from ground on which they are formed.

BATTEN: Long, thin piece of squared timber used for flooring or hanging roof tiles.

BAYS: Internal compartments of a building; each divided from the other not by solid walls but by divisions only marked in the side walls. Also external divisions of a building by fenestration.

BELVEDERE: Raised turret from which to view scenery.

BILLET MOULDING: Ornamental moulding consisting of small cylindrical blocks arranged in a sunk moulding.

BUCRANE: Sculptured ornament representing ox skull.

BUTTRESS: Projecting support built on to outside of wall.

CABOCHONS: Precious stones polished but not cut into facets.

CADUCEUS: Mercury's wand.

Calderium: Hot rooms in Roman baths.

CALIFAL: Associated with the rule of the Caliph.

CALOTTE: Flattened dome: skull cap.

CALVARY: Open air representation of the Crucifixion.

CAMPANILE: Isolated bell-tower.

CAPITAL: Moulded or carved top of column.

CARYATID: Whole figure supporting an entablature or other similar member.

CASEMATE: Vaulted chamber in thickness of fortress-wall, with embrasures for defence.

CENSE: The act of burning incense.

CENSER: A vessel in which incense is burned.

CHALICE: Cup used in Communion service or at Mass.

Chambranle: Door casing.

CHAMFER: Surface produced by bevelling square edge or corner equally on both sides—moulding.

CHAMPLEVÉ ENAMEL: Work in which the metal ground is hollowed out and spaces filled with enamel.

CHAPTER HOUSE: Meeting place of members of religious order.

CHASUBLE: The outer vestment of the celebrant at Mass.

CHEVET: Apsidal east end of medieval church.

CHRISMA: A monogram of Christ formed by the letters χ and ρ.

CIBORIUM: Vessel similar to chalice in which the Host is deposited. Canopy over high altar.

CINQUEFOIL: Arch or circular opening divided into five lobes or leaves by projecting carving.

CIPOLIN (marble): Green-veined marble from the island of Euboea.

CIPPUS: Roman term for monumental pillar.

CISTERCIAN: Order founded in 1098 in Burgundy, at Cîteaux (Latin *Cistercium*) near Dijon, and which received a great impulse under St. Bernard, founder of the Abbey of Clairvaux. The monasteries of this Order express by their architecture the severity of the rule (more austere form of Benedictine rule).

CLERESTORY: Upper storey with rows of windows.

COFFER: Deep panel in ceiling, vault or dome.

CONSOLE: Ornamental bracket used to support cornice on which to place busts, vases or figures.

COPE: Ecclesiastical vestment worn over surplice.

CORBEL: Block of stone projecting from a wall, supporting some horizontal feature.

CORNICE: Uppermost member of entablature, surmounting the frieze.

COSMATO: Mosaic work of coloured marble.

COUNTERSCARP: Outer wall or slope of ditch, supporting covered way.

CRENEL: Open space of a battlement.

CROCKET: Carved ornament on angles of spires and on canopies.

CROSSING: That part of a cruciform church where the transepts cross the nave.

CUFIC: Pertaining to Cufa, a town on the Euphrates, south of Babylon; applied especially to an Arabic alphabet earlier employed there.

CULVERIN: Small firearm; large cannon, very long in proportion to its bore, used especially in 16th and 17th centuries.

CUPOLA: Spherical vault or concave ceiling.

CYCLOPEAN: Style of masonry with walls of large, irregular stones, unhewn and uncemented, which in ancient Greece were fabled to be the work of Cyclopes, or one-eyed giants.

DOLMEN: Megalithic tomb, large flat stone laid horizontally upon upright ones.

DRIP-STONE: Projecting moulding to throw off rain.

DRUM OR TAMBOUR: Upright part of a cupola.

Enceinte: An enclosing wall of fortifications.

ENGAGED: Built into. ENGAGED COLUMN: Column built into wall.

ENTABLATURE: Arrangement of horizontal members above supporting columns.

ENTASIS: Convex tapering of a column.

EPISTLE SIDE OR ALTAR: Right side.

EXEDRA: Apsidal end of a room.

EXTRADOS: Outer curve of arch.

FAÇADE: Face or front of building.

FAÏENCE: Decorated glazed earthenware.

FINIAL: Ornamental feature placed on top of pinnacle or at base and apex of gable.

FLAMBOYANT: Late form of the Gothic style, characteristic for its "florid" enrichments of carved ornament, and for the "flaming" arrangements of the window stone-filling.

FLUTING: Vertical channelling in the shaft of a column.

FOIL: Lobe formed by the cusping of a circle or an arch. Trefoil, quatrefoil, cinquefoil, multifoil, express number of leaf shapes to be seen.

FOLIATED: Carved with leaf shapes.

FRESCO: Painting on plastered wall before plaster has dried.

FRIEZE: Middle division of a classical entablature.

GALLERY: In church architecture, upper storey above an aisle, opened in arches to the nave.

GALLO-ROMAN: Belonging to the epoch when Gaul was a part of the Roman Empire (1st–4th century).

GLACIS: Bank sloping down from fort, on which attackers are without cover from gunfire.

GOTHIC: Style which appeared in France in the 12th century, and prevailed in Europe from the 13th to the 15th century. Its chief elements are the vault with diagonal ribs with pointed arches and flying buttresses.

GROIN: Sharp edge at the meeting of two cells of a cross-vault.

HELICOIDAL: Resembling a snail shell; spiral ornament.

HENNIN: A high, conical head-dress with a muslin veil worn by fashionable ladies in the 15th century.

HIERATISM: Priestly tradition that made Byzantine art too rigid.

HIGH GOTHIC: *see* Flamboyant.

HISTORIATED: Adorned with figures.

Hôtel: Large house or mansion, in addition to meaning as in English hotel.

IMBRICATED: Overlapping.

IMPOST: Brackets in walls, usually formed of mouldings, on which the ends of an arch rest.

In commendum: Ecclesiastical benefice temporarily held in care of clerk.

INTAGLIO: Engraved design; incised carving in hard material.

INTRADOS: Inner curve or underside of an arch.

JAMB: Straight side of an archway, doorway, or window.

JUBE: Screen between nave and chancel (rood-screen).

LANCET: Tall, narrow window with acutely pointed head.

LANTERN: In architecture, a small circular or polygonal turret with windows all round crowning a roof or dome.

LIERNE: Short rib connecting two main ribs.

LINTEL: Horizontal beam or stone bridging an opening.

LOMBARD: Early form of the Romanesque style (9th and 10th centuries) born in Lombardy, Italy.

LOZENGE: Diamond shape.

MACHICOLATION: Projecting gallery or parapet with series of openings for pouring molten substances on attackers below.

MANDORLA: Almond-shaped oval around figure in a painting.

MANSARD: Form of curb roof in which each face of the roof has two slopes, the lower being steeper than the other. Named after the French architect, François Mansard (1598–1666).

MARQUETRY: Inlaid work arranged to form decorative patterns.

MERLON: Part of wall of battlement lying between two openings.

Mezzo-rilievo: Degree of relief in figures halfway between high and low.

MINIATURE: Painting on a very small scale.

Mirador: Balcony.

MISERERE: Projection on underside of tilt-up seat in choir-stall.

MISERICORD: Room set apart in monastery where monks might take special food as an indulgence: the indulgence or relaxation of monastic rule itself.

MODILLION: Projecting bracket under a cornice in Corinthian and other orders.

MULLION: Vertical bar of wood or stone dividing window into two or more "lights".

NARTHEX: In early Christian architecture, a vestibule forming an entrance to a basilica, originally for women penitents and catechumens.

NAVE: Body of church.

NEWEL: Central post in circular or winding staircase; also principal post when flight of stairs meets a landing.

NIMBUS: Bright cloud or halo investing deity or saint.

Nymphaeum: Roman temple of the nymphs.

OCULUS: Circular or "bull's-eye" window.

OGIVE: Pointed arch or window, with double curve.

Oppidum: Latin for town.

ORDER: In classic architecture, column with base, shaft, capital, and entablature according to one of the following styles: Greek Doric, Roman Doric, Tuscan Doric, Ionic, Corinthian, Composite. Alternatively an Order of monks.

OSSUARY: Receptacle for bones of the dead.

OVEN-SHAPED: This description is applied to the structures which have the dome shape of the old French bread ovens, e.g. mainly in the case of apses at the eastern end of the church.

PARADOS: Elevation of earth behind fortified place to secure it from rear attack.

PARVIS: Enclosed area in front of church or cathedral.

PATERA: Small flat circular or oval ornament in classical architecture.

PATINA: Bowl or pan. Encrustation of age to works of art.

PATIO: Courtyard.

PEDIMENT: Low-pitched gable used in classical, Renaissance, and neo-classical architecture above a portico.

PENDENTIVE: Spherical triangle formed between each pair of supporting arches in dome resting on square base.

PERISTYLE: Row of columns round building or courtyard.

PHALANSTERY: The dwelling of the phalange in ideal social system of Fourier (1772–1837).

Pietà: A representation of the Virgin Mary mourning over the dead body of Christ.

Pieve: Parish church.

PILASTER: Flat column against face of wall.

PINNACLE: Ornamental form crowning a spire, tower, buttress.

PISCINA: Basin for washing the Communion or Mass vessels.

PLATERESQUE: Extremely florid and decorative style of architecture (from *plateria*—silverwork) with minuteness of detail.

POLYPTYCH: Picture or carving with many panels.

PORTAL: Gate or doorway.

PREDELLA: In an altar-piece the horizontal strip below the main representation, often used for a number of subsidiary representations in a row.

PRESBYTERY: Part of church reserved for clergy, also dwelling house for clergy.

PRONAOS: Space in front of body of temple enclosed by portico and projecting side walls.

PSALTER: Book of Psalms.

Putto (plural *putti*): Small naked boy.

PYXIS: Sacred box containing Host after consecration.

RAMPART: Defensive bank of earth, with or without stone parapet.

RELIQUARIES: Chests or caskets containing relics.

Rocca: Fortress.

ROCOCO: Late Baroque style with a profusion of rock-like forms, scrolls, crimped shells (from French "rocaille" —"rock work").

ROMANESQUE: Architectural style prevalent in Western Europe towards the end of 12th century, characterised by use of massive stone vaulting and the round-headed arch. Usually known in reference to English buildings as Norman.

ROOD-SCHEEN: Open screen across chancel entrance in church.

ROSE-WINDOW: Gothic circular window filled with tracery resembling a rose.

ROTUNDA: Circular building, usually with doomed roof.
RUPESTRAL: Rock.

SACRISTY: Part of church where sacred vessels and vestments are kept.
SARCOPHAGUS: Stone receptacle for corpse.
SERPENTINE: Decorative stone.
SOFFIT: Underside of lintel, arch or cornice.
SPRINGER: Bottom stone of arch.
SQUINCH: Small stone arch across an interior angle of square tower to support octagonal spire.
STEREOTOMY: Art or science of cutting stones into regular forms.
STRINGCOURSE: Projecting horizontal moulding or projecting course of stone or brick running across face of building.
STUCCO: Plaster work.

TELAMONES: Carved male figures serving as pillars.
TIERCERON: Secondary rib, issuing from main springer or central boss and leading to a ridge rib.
TORUS: Moulding in base of columns with semi-circular profile.
TRANSEPT: Transverse portion of a cross-shaped church.
TRANSOM: Horizontal bar across the openings of a window.
TRAVERTINE: A variety of limestone found near Tivoli.
TRIBUNAL: Confessional.
TRIBUNE: Gallery of church.
TRIFORIUM: Arcaded wall passage or blank arcading facing the nave at the height of the roof of the side-aisles and below the clerestory windows.
TRIPTYCH: Picture or carving on three panels.
TUFA: Rock of cellular texture of volcanic origin.
TYMPANUM: Triangular space between sloping and horizontal cornices above lintel of doorway.

VOLUTE: Spiral scroll.

WAGON-ROOF: Roof in which by closely set rafters with
   arched braces the appearance of the inside of a canvas
   tilt over a wagon is achieved.

INDEX OF TOWNS AND PLACES VISITED